David Smith is a solicitor specialising in residential property, agency, and regulatory law. He is a partner at JMW Solicitors LLP in London. He is well known for his work in the residential property and agency field, especially in property licensing and consumer law and has advised local and national governments, large and small landlords and tenants and letting and estate agents across the sector. He has worked extensively in the devolved governments as they have developed their own residential tenancy law and retains a fascination with the different approaches to residential property in different parts of the UK and internationally.

A Practical Guide to the Law of Private Renting in Northern Ireland

A Practical Guide to the Law of Private Renting in Northern Ireland

David Stuart Nicholas Smith
Solicitor (England and Wales)
BSc (Econ), LLB, PhD (Wales)

Law Brief Publishing

Published 2021 by Law Brief Publishing, an imprint of Law Brief Publishing Ltd
30 The Parks
Minehead
Somerset
TA24 8BT

www.lawbriefpublishing.com

Paperback: 978-1-913715-50-2

For my wife and daughter with love and gratitude for their continued patience

PREFACE

It might reasonably be asked what business a solicitor from England and Wales has writing a book about residential letting law in Northern Ireland. To that I have two responses.

First, I have followed the twists and turns of the legislation since it was first discussed and know as much about it as anyone. This text started out after a client asked me to provide a brief introduction to the law private lettings in Northern Ireland for people who understood the PRS in England and Wales. It then became a notepad of sorts as I continued to explore and observe the development of the law. One benefit of new legislation is that there is little case law and so there is more ability to look at it from afar without much "on the ground" experience and still be able to comment usefully.

Secondly, Northern Ireland is a relatively small jurisdiction. It has a very small body of case law on residential housing reflecting both its limited size and the small size of the residential letting market within it.

Thirdly, legislation in Northern Ireland often shares concepts, and often entire chunks of wording, with legislation from other parts of the United Kingdom. This occurs because of the hiring of legislative drafters from other UK jurisdictions, communication between drafters in different parts of the UK, the fact that some parts of the legislation were drafted in Westminster and made using executive powers, and also the simple reality of it being easier for time-poor drafters to borrow a passage from another jurisdiction than write one from scratch themselves! However, this means that case law and commentary on legislation from other parts of the UK are frequently relevant to Norther Ireland and so a book written by an outsider who is familiar with those other pieces of legislation can still add value. This argument should be treated with a degree of scepticism however. A similar proposition could be advanced for any of the smaller jurisdictions of the United Kingdom and, if correct, would reduce them to little more than satellites of Westminster Parliament. The fact that the same wording has been used in multiple jurisdictions does not mean that it was intended to have the same effect in those jurisdictions.

Of course, the real truth is, as my long-suffering wife will attest, that I am endlessly fascinated by residential landlord and tenant law and the many similarities and differences in the approach adopted by different jurisdictions to quite similar issues. The United Kingdom provides a particularly interesting perspective on this as several jurisdictions with common legal underpinnings have, through the magic of devolution, been given the opportunity to take entirely different legal and policy approaches to housing problems that are remarkably similar. Therefore, they function as a real-time research environment as different approaches can be compared and contrasted and their effects examined.

The various online resources made available by the Northern Irish government, Northern Ireland Law Society, local authorities and judiciary have been an invaluable resource in putting this book together and they have my thanks. The friends and colleagues who have helped me develop as a solicitor and influenced my thinking to lead to books like this have also been invaluable and my gratitude to them goes beyond mere words. As always, any errors are mine alone.

The law is correct as at 15 December 2020.

David Smith
December 2020

CONTENTS

CHAPTER ONE

LEGAL SYSTEM IN NORTHERN IRELAND

To understand the legal system in Northern Ireland it is necessary to know a little of its legal history which is a reflection of the difficult political history of the provinces. The waxing and waning of English influence has left its mark in the legal history and practice of Northern Ireland.

In early times Ireland had its own native system of law and custom known as Brehon law which was created and applied by native jurists known as Brehons. After the invasion of the Normans the imposition of English Law spread across Ireland pushing out the Brehon system. However, the reduction of English influence in the period up until approximately 1500 led to a consequent loss of influence of English law and the Brehon system reasserted itself.

Under the Tudors the reconquest of Ireland led to a destruction of the Brehon law system and its supplanting by English Law and the Brehon system has had practically no influence since. The system in Ireland has, since then, closely followed the development of the common law system of England and Wales (and probably more accurately mirrors it than the Scottish system). After the partition of Ireland in 1921 there was an inevitable divergence between the law in North and South with the North staying closer to its British origins and the South seeing variation due to the creation of a constitution and its different Parliament but, in property matters, there remains a surprising similarity between the two parts of Ireland and there are key pieces of legislation from before 1921 that continue to apply.

Law Making

As with the rest of the UK the primary source of Law in Northern Ireland is the Parliament in Westminster. It is responsible for passing Acts of Parliament which are supplemented by Statutory Instruments. In the devolved areas then the devolved bodies have similar powers under certain specific limits. Ultimately, it is the Westminster Parliament, by passing Acts, which has permitted transfer of limited powers to devolved bodies.

When considering Acts of Parliament it is important to distinguish between those that apply to the whole UK or just to specific parts of it. Some legislation applies just to England and Wales, while other legislation will also apply wholly or partly to Northern Ireland or Scotland.

In Northern Ireland there is another key source of law. During periods prior to the creation of the Northern Ireland Assembly or when it has been in suspension then much legislation has been passed 'in Council'. This has allowed the Secretary of State for Northern Ireland to exercise substantial control over the province directly with very limited review of the legislation being passed, and that being conducted entirely in Westminster by committees of the House of Commons and Lords. Legislation has therefore been drawn up by civil servants and ministers and passed straight into law with almost no input, and certainly no local input.

Due to the process of drawing up Orders in Council law in Northern Ireland has often found itself proceeding in fits and starts as the executive turns its mind to various topics. In less crucial areas like housing the law has often also been 'borrowed' from previous legislation that has passed effectively through Parliament. This has led to a somewhat patchwork set of legislation for Northern Ireland but has also meant that parts of the law prove recognisable to practitioners with an England and Wales background and provide a ready ground for interpretation provided by Courts in England and Wales to work in.

Devolution

The legal system in Northern Ireland is complicated by the devolution of powers from Parliament to other elected and non-elected bodies. In the past most powers have been exercised directly by the Northern Ireland Office under authority granted by a number of Acts.[1] Currently, certain powers are devolved to the Northern Ireland Assembly under the terms of the Northern Ireland Act 1998.

The power of the Assembly is strictly limited. It is only authorised to pass Acts in certain areas. Acts of the Northern Ireland Assembly are also subject to review by the Courts and can be struck down if they are found to be outside the authority granted to the Assembly, if they violate EU law[2] or the European Convention on Human Rights, or if they discriminate against individuals on the grounds of political opinion or religious belief. In addition any bill passed by the Assembly must be approved by the Secretary of State for Northern Ireland before receiving Royal Assent and he will refuse to submit a bill to the monarch for Assent if he believes that it exceeds the Assembly's powers. If submitted by the Secretary of State, the monarch will sign a bill into law.

Case law and application

Due to the chequered history of Northern Ireland it draws its judicial case law from several different sources. Naturally the primary source is from the legal decisions of the High Court in Belfast and the Court of Appeal and House of Lords when ruling on matters of Northern Ireland law where the normal doctrine of judicial precedent will be followed.

As is normal with other UK jurisdictions, decisions made in the other jurisdictions are also relevant. However, Northern Irish courts have tended to follow higher courts made in relation to England and Wales or Scottish matters unless there is some specific Northern Ireland context

[1] Most recently the Northern Ireland (Temporary Provisions) Act 1972.

[2] It is unclear how this requirement will change as a result of Brexit.

that suggests they should not do so. Therefore, Supreme Court decisions will bind Courts in Northern Ireland irrespective of which jurisdiction they are ruling under and will also supersede conflicting decisions made by the Court of Appeal ruling on Northern Ireland matters. Court of Appeal decisions made in England and Wales will also be accorded extreme respect in Northern Ireland and they will generally be followed by all lower Courts and the Northern Ireland Court of Appeal will only depart from them when it has very good reason to do so. Equally, the Northern Ireland High Court will accord great respect to decisions made by the England and Wales High Court. Where a decision is made by the High Court or Court of Appeal of Ireland on a piece of legislation that predates the partition it will also be accorded respect and will be followed where the law is sufficiently similar.

This is particularly so when the wording of legislation is similar. Historically Northern Irish lettings legislation was written by civil servants and passed into law by the Northern Ireland minister using direct powers. As a result, much of it has been a direct copy of components of legislation written in England. This means that senior court rulings made in England carry especial weight in Northern Ireland as they often are about pieces of wording which are the same or very similar. The growth in power of the Northern Irish Assembly has eroded this aspect to a degree as a legislative style and wording which is more unique to Northern Ireland comes to be developed.

Overview of Landlord and Tenant Law in Northern Ireland

Residential landlord and tenant law in Northern Ireland did not develop rapidly for much of the 20th Century. The distraction of security issues and the lack of functioning local democracy meant that the narrow concerns of Westminster politicians held sway and so housing issues were not of great concern. Until relatively recently lettings operated largely on the basis of 1970s legislation[3] which was similar to legislation from the

[3] Rent (Northern Ireland) Order 1978.

same period in England and Wales.[4] Tenancies that fell outside the scope of this legislation were almost totally uncontrolled and tenants of these premises had few rights. Therefore rental activity tended to be confined to social landlords and the private rental sector was underdeveloped.

Where We Are Today

There has been a building pressure to reform the sector in Northern Ireland due to the economic benefits of peace and stability. Large inward investment has occurred in all sectors, including housing, and the limitations imposed by the law were preventing growth. There has also been a desire to modernise and improve housing and a recognition that this is best achieved by stimulating the private market. Therefore, there has been a desire to liberalise the tenancy position to encourage private landlords but this has been coupled with a desire to ensure that existing properties are modernised and improved.

The creation of a devolved assembly, albeit one that has had substantial periods when it was suspended, has reinvigorated the approach and a significant amount of change has occurred in a relatively short time, modernising the PRS and introducing a range of legislation which mirrors aspects of other parts of the United Kingdom but which is also unique to Northern Ireland.

However, Northern Ireland currently finds itself operating with a Byzantine mix of legislation made by Order by, not always very engaged, Northern Ireland Ministers using their direct powers; legislation made by Order of Northern Ireland Ministers during periods when the Northern Ireland Assembly was suspended, which often took Bills passing through the Assembly in whatever form they had reached and made them law as they stood at that point; and full Acts of the Northern Ireland Assembly made after more substantial debate and consideration.

[4] Rent Act 1977.

CHAPTER TWO

PRIVATE TENANCIES

The Private Tenancies (Northern Ireland) Order 2006 (the "2006 Order") has been a key element in the growth of the private rented sector in Northern Ireland. It was not the only driver of that growth, which began in the 1990s as the peace dividend and the revival of the Northern Ireland economy was bolstered by a supply of relatively cheap lending secured on residential property along with the beginning of the house price rises that have continued ever since.[5] However, just as the Housing Act 1988 created a legal framework which bolstered the rise of the PRS in England and Wales, the 2006 Order put the PRS in Northern Ireland on a firm footing.

It has had an unusual gestation. It found its origins in work carried out by the Northern Ireland Department for Social Development and the Northern Ireland Housing Executive who published a joint strategy for the private rented sector in May 2004.[6] The overall aim of that strategy was to promote and sustain a healthy private rented sector, offering choice and flexibility by influencing supply and securing a better quality, managed sector. The Northern Ireland Assembly had however been suspended since 2002 and so the proposals were eventually implemented by way of an order in council with a minimal level of scrutiny in sub-committees of the Houses of Parliament. To be fair this was recognised at the time with David Hanson MP, then a Minister of State for the Northern Ireland Office, acknowledging the unsatisfactory and hugely abbreviated consideration being given to the Order as

[5] Karly Greene and Heather Porter, "A place apart? Trends and challenges in the Northern Ireland housing market" Housing Finance International Spring 2018.

[6] Renting Privately—A Strategic Framework.

compared to what would have occurred in a properly constituted Northern Ireland Assembly.[7]

The exact purpose of the Order is not wholly clear. In debate the Minister of State for Northern Ireland suggested that the order would bring Northern Ireland legislation on the PRS closer to that found in England and Wales.[8] However, this is very definitely not what occurred. In fact, Northern Ireland was already quite close to the way things were in England & Wales before the 2006 Order. It was just that it was close to the system that operated in England & Wales prior to the introduction of the Housing Act 1988. A number of residential tenancies were afforded very significant protection while the remainder had almost no protection at all. The Order however did not move Northern Ireland closer to where England had gone as it in no way replicates the Housing Act 1988. Rather, it drew on a mix of concepts from England and Wales and Scotland as well as using unique ideas of its own to create a blend which is entirely unique to Northern Ireland.

Unusually, compared with the rest of the UK, the 2006 Order has remained the cornerstone of the PRS in Northern Ireland. A substantial amount of the legislation since has simply amended the Order or added segments into it and the Order has therefore served something of a consolidating function. Tenancy deposit protection and landlord registration for example have both been grafted into the Order. By contrast, elsewhere in the UK more and more legislation has been layered on top of existing structures creating a confusing patchwork with little effort being made to consolidate them in a meaningful manner.

When the Assembly returned in 2007 much effort was devoted to work on the PRS and other parts of the housing sector. A lot of change was made in 2011[9] which represented a substantial reframing of the 2006

[7] Draft Private Tenancies (Northern Ireland) Order 2006 Deb 10 May 2006 c6.

[8] Draft Private Tenancies (Northern Ireland) Order 2006 Deb 10 May 2006 c8.

[9] By the Housing (Amendment) Act (Northern Ireland) 201.

Order and control over housing being brought definitively back within the control of the Northern Ireland Assembly.

However, the pace of change in Northern Ireland has since dropped off as the Assembly has moved through a further period of suspension while other parts of the UK have pushed ahead with ambitious reform.[10]

The 2006 Order is fairly light touch in its operation. It does not create a full tenancy regime itself as previous legislation did[11] and focuses instead on creating an underpinning structure which permits a substantial degree of freedom of contract and only steps in to create certain minimum standards or fill in gaps left by the contract. It therefore tried to work in concert with the manner in which the Northern Irish sector had been developing prior to its coming into effect by seeking to tame the more wild aspects of its character rather than seeking to re-impose the highly structured regime of the late 1970's. In fact, much of the work since then has been focused on hanging more regulation onto that initial framework to bring the Northern Irish PRS towards the more regulated model being operated in the rest of the UK. However, the PRS in Northern Ireland still retains a strong element of contractual freedom, more so than the rest of the UK, which is slowly being brought under tighter control. As the interests of the Northern Ireland Assembly often follow those of other law making bodies in the UK this has meant that there is considerable control in some areas and very little in others. No doubt, this will change over time as the gaps are filled in.

The 2006 Order only applies to tenancies. Therefore, if an occupation is not a tenancy (if it is a licence, for example) then the protections afforded by the Order will not apply. This makes the tenancy versus licence

[10] Wendy Wilson et al, Comparing private rented sector policies in England, Scotland, Wales and Northern Ireland, House of Commons Library Briefing Paper, 19/07624, 2 May 2019, p. 4.

[11] Rent (Northern Ireland) Order 1978.

debate, which arises with increasing frequency in all UK jurisdictions no less important in Northern Ireland. The Order also does not apply to:

- tenancies for more than 99 years;
- tenancies granted by the crown or to a government department (both Northern Ireland government departments and UK ones);
- tenancies granted by the NIHE or a housing association; or
- holiday lettings.

As is common in other UK jurisdictions there is no clear definition of a holiday letting. In England the courts have held that it is the intention of the parties at the time that the tenancy was granted and so each case will turn on its fact. The wording on the agreement is a useful indicator of what the parties intended but it can be displaced by evidence of the facts on the ground.[12]

The Order sets out certain basic requirements that landlords must fulfil in terms of giving information. As originally drafted the landlord was required to provide a tenant with a full statement of the terms of their tenancy and a set of statutorily prescribed wording telling them about their rights but this obligation was repealed.[13] However, the second requirement, to give the tenant a rent book remains.[14] The rent book is required to contain certain information which is prescribed.[15] This is:

- the property address;

[12] *Buchmann v May* [1978] 2 All E.R. 993.

[13] By s1, Housing (Amendment) Act (Northern Ireland) 2011.

[14] Article 5, 2006 Order.

[15] By the Rent Book Regulations (Northern Ireland) 2007.

- the tenant's name;
- the landlord's name, address and telephone and the same for their agent if they have one;
- the rent and the payment periods;
- the capital value of the property, the rates payable, and whether those rates are included in the rent;
- any other payment that the tenant is required to make; and
- the start date of the tenancy.

This requirement is something of an anachronism. It was in fact something of an anachronism at the time the Order was made as most tenants were already paying their rent by bank transfer at that time, a trend that has hardly reversed itself! The outmoded nature of this idea was raised several times during the House of Lords during the committee debate on the Order. However, the government minister concerned dismissed the points asserting that a rent book provided some degree of proof of the payment of rent.[16] This seems a rather odd idea since a bank transfer has its own in-built form of evidence and it has ended up raising the question, never satisfactorily answered, of what a landlord is supposed to do to keep the rent book up to date with payments that they have received electronically from the tenant. In some cases, agents simply electronically generate a new rent book periodically and send it to the tenant so the document ends up becoming more of a written statement of account.

The 2006 Order also largely ends the protected and statutory tenancy regime in Northern Ireland.[17] The 2006 Order prevents the creation of

[16] Draft Private Tenancies (Northern Ireland) Order 2006 HL Deb, 17 May 2006, c345.

[17] Created by the Rent (Northern Ireland) Order 1978.

any new protected tenancies[18] and additionally limits the succession rights under the old regime so that these tenancies will reduce in number. Due to this I have chosen not to cover the older regime in this text.

Tenancy deposits

Tenancy deposit protection provisions were inserted into the 2006 Order in 2011.[19] The provisions inserted into the Order were relatively lightweight and only set out the barest outlines of a deposit scheme. The actual scheme was brought into effect later in 2012.[20] However, the requirement to protect a deposit only came into effect on 1 April 2013 when four schemes (reduced to three shortly afterwards) were approved by the Northern Ireland government. Therefore, the provisions only apply to new tenancies started from that date.

The actual provisions are fairly similar to those operated in England and Wales[21] in that they focus on the receipt of funds intended to be used as security for the performance of an obligation under the tenancy and it is this receipt which triggers the obligation on the landlord.

There are in fact three obligations, to protect the deposit with an authorised scheme within 14 days from receiving the deposit, comply with the initial requirements of such a scheme in the same time period, and given the tenant the information prescribed by law[22] within 28 days of receipt of the deposit. The Court of Appeal in England has held that all these requirements are of equal importance and it is not open to a landlord to point to the fact that the deposit is protected and say that the tenant can get all the other information they need from the relevant

[18] Article 5.

[19] By way of the Housing (Amendment) Act (Northern Ireland) 2011.

[20] By the Tenancy Deposit Schemes Regulations (Northern Ireland) 2012.

[21] In ss212-217, Housing Act 2004.

[22] In Schedule 1, Tenancy Deposit Schemes Regulations (Northern Ireland) 2012.

scheme website for themselves.[23] It is worth noting that the date for compliance is based on the date the deposit was taken and not the start date of the tenancy. This can cause problems with tenancies that are due to start some way into the future, such as student tenancies, if the deposit is taken much earlier. In relation to the "initial requirements" of a deposit scheme there has never been any clarity as to what that means save that the English High Court has held that schemes cannot use this to "gold plate" the statutory obligations and it seems to be more of a reference to landlords registering the deposit properly using whatever clerical mechanism the relevant scheme requires.[24] In relation, to the definition of a deposit the requirement is that it must be paid as security for another obligation rather than in discharge of an obligation itself. So, rent in advance cannot be a deposit as it is intended to discharge the obligation to pay rent rather than acting as security.[25]

However, a key difference in the Northern Ireland scheme is that enforcement in by way of prosecution or civil penalty levied by a local authority. This is distinctly different from other UK jurisdictions which allow for civil claims by tenants and give them an incentive to do so by allowing them to claim a multiple of up to three times the original deposit sum. There has been consideration given in Northern Ireland to adopting this mechanism as well. Currently the maximum penalty is three times the deposit sum but this is retained entirely by the state. Proposals have been made to give the tenant some of this money to give them direct recompense and, presumably also to incentivise them to report breaches.[26] The fact that this is a criminal penalty in Norther Ireland has meant that local authorities are less likely to take action in the case of minor breaches where there has been no suffering on the part of the tenant, such as registering slightly late. In England and Wales, the fact

---

[23] *Ayannuga v Swindells* [2012] EWCA Civ 1789.

[24] *Draycott & Draycott v Hannells Letting Limited* [2010] EWHC 217

[25] *Johnson & Ors v Old* [2013] EWCA Civ 415.

[26] Department for Communities, Private Rented Sector in Northern Ireland – Proposals for Change, Consultation Document January 2017.

that a tenant can recover a significant sum of money for such minor errors has led to a substantial amount of litigation which has led to rapid development of the law.

Term and termination

The 2006 Order effectively abolished tenancies that were periodic from commencement, ordering that any tenancy which was not granted for a fixed term would be deemed to be granted for a six-month fixed term.[27] The Order has also created a somewhat unique approach to notice periods. Previously the common law position of a notice to quit being the same as one period of the tenancy had applied in Northern Ireland. The Order initially placed a four-week minimum notice period in place. However, it was later amended[28] to create a minimum notice period that varied according to the time for which the tenancy has been in place. These are:

Tenancy Length	Minimum notice period
less than 5 years	4 weeks
between 5 and 10 years	8 weeks
more than 10 years	12 weeks

Compared to other parts of the UK these notice periods are still not hugely generous and few tenants in the private sector will actually be able to avail themselves of the longer notice periods as their tenancies are unlikely to last that long. However, the concept of notice periods that become longer for longer tenancies is one that is unique in the UK. There are proposals to increase the notice period for all tenancies lasting more

[27] Article 13.

[28] By s3, Housing (Amendment) Act (Northern Ireland) 2011.

than 12 months from 4 weeks up to 12 months. There are also proposals to structure the eviction process better to mimic that set out in England[29] with specific breaches leading to mandatory possession, removing the discretion of the court, and having these more severe cases dealt with largely on paper.[30]

During the Covid-19 pandemic the notice period was altered on a temporary basis so that all tenants were able to avail themselves of a 12-week notice period[31] and also allowed the notice period to be extended by secondary legislation up to a maximum of six months and to enable the longer notice period to run longer than the one provided for in the Act.[32]

The new termination provisions only apply to termination on the basis of a notice to quit. In England it has always been the case that a notice it quit is not required to determine a fixed term tenancy which clearly expresses an end date.[33] Therefore it is doubtful whether any protection accrues to a fixed term tenant at the end of their tenancy.

Equally, the 2006 Order does not appear to impact the common law of forfeiture at all. There is no equivalent provisions in the Order to those which continue or renew tenancies as long as the tenant remains in occupation[34] and only permit the court to make possession orders for

---

[29] In the Housing Act 1988.

[30] Department for Communities, Private Rented Sector in Northern Ireland – Proposals for Change, Consultation Document January 2017.

[31] Section 1, Private Tenancies (Coronavirus Modifications) Act (Northern Ireland) 2020.

[32] 30 September 2020 but extended to 31 March 2021 by the Private Tenancies (Coronavirus Modifications) Regulations (Northern Ireland) 2020.

[33] *Right d. Flower v. Darby* (1786) 1 T.R. 159, 162.

[34] Section 4, Rent (Northern Ireland) Order 1978 or in England s5, Housing Act 1988.

specified grounds.[35] So the provisions as to the termination of a tenancy for a breach of the agreement will rely on the terms of that agreement. There are a number of advisors suggesting that a landlord must serve a notice to quit under the Order for breaches of the tenancy agreement. The advice from the Northern Ireland government around Covid-19 appears to suggest that eviction of a tenant for rent arrears requires a notice to quit. My view is that this cannot be correct either as a matter of law or as simple logic. The common law right to forfeit exists unless there is some specific mechanism which blocks it, no such mechanism exists within the Order. The provisions as to notices to quit do not apply to forfeiture which is a distinct legal remedy. As to practicality, the 2006 Order effectively prohibits the service of a notice to quit in the first six months of a tenancy as a common law notice to quit cannot be served inside a fixed term. It cannot possibly be intended that a landlord would have to accept a situation where their tenant could accrue rent arrears during the first six months of a tenancy with no effective means of redress. Therefore, unless the notice to quit provisions in the Order are intended to refer to some free-standing statutory notice mechanism as opposed to imposing controls on common law notices to quit, the provisions cannot apply to forfeiture for breach.

In addition, the wording of the relevant article[36] suggests a limit to its intended application. It states that is applies to a "notice by a landlord or tenant to quit a dwelling-house" must be in writing and give a specified time period. The equivalent statute in England and Wales which sets a minimum time period for a notice to quit[37] also uses the very similar phrasing "notice by a landlord or a tenant to quit any premises" when discussing validity. In addition, the relevant legislation requiring a court order to possess a residential dwelling specifically includes a provision stating that any residential lease which contains a right of re-entry or

---

[35] Section 13, Rent (Northern Ireland) Order 1978 or in England s8, Housing Act 1988.

[36] Article 14.

[37] Section 5, Protection From Eviction Act 1977.

forfeiture cannot have that right acted on without appropriate court proceedings.[38] This would seem to indicate that the legislation does continue to anticipate a right to forfeiture in tenancy agreements independent of the use of Notices to Quit.

However, it seems clear that the Northern Ireland government is of the view that a notice to terminate a tenancy for a breach must comply with this part of the 2006 Order.

If there is no requirement for a notice to quit and accordingly the minimum notice period does not apply then the introduction of the 2006 Order somewhat winds the clock back on termination for breach of lease terms in Northern Ireland.[39] Tenants who have failed to pay their rent in breach of covenant have almost no protection other than that provided for by the terms of their tenancy. Tenants who are in breach of a provision other than one involving payment of rent can probably rely on the statutory requirement that they be given a notice specifying the breach, requiring compensation, and giving a reasonable period to remedy the breach.[40] It seems likely that a court might hold in such a case that the reasonable period required was similar to that specified by the Order ,[41] thereby bringing back the notice provisions in the 2006 Order by the back door. But this would not avail a tenant in rent arrears who would have no more protection than that afforded by the common law of forfeiture and the wording of his or her tenancy agreement.[42]

Unlawful eviction and Harassment

There are restrictions in Northern Ireland, as there are in most UK jurisdictions and elsewhere as well, on evicting tenants without allowing

---

[38] Article 55, Rent (Northern Ireland) Order 1978.

[39] As compared to the position under the Rent (Northern Ireland) Order 1978.

[40] Section 14, Conveyancing and Law of Property Act 1881.

[41] In Article 13, 2006 Order.

[42] As s14 of the 1881 Act does not apply in these cases.

for a proper court process. The 2006 Order has modified[43] the original law on the issues of eviction and harassment but not considerably.[44]

There is a generalised prohibition on the eviction of someone who is occupying a dwelling-house on the basis of a tenancy or who is occupying it lawfully by way of rights derived through that tenancy (an authorised sub-tenant for example) other than through the court. These provisions mimic precisely those in England and Wales.[45] In England, the courts have held that the prohibition extends not just to properties let wholly as residential dwellings but also to premises that have been let partly for business use alongside their residential use.[46] The English legislation differs in that it explicitly includes licences within the scope of protection. This has led to further cases on whether hotels and local authority temporary accommodation were included. However, the Northern Ireland legislation has no explicit inclusion of a licence and so it would seem that residential licences have little or no protection. However, where a person has exclusive possession of premises as a consequence of his employment then he also gains the protection of these provisions, even if he is not in fact a tenant.[47]

In addition to the prohibitions on eviction without court proceedings there are further prohibitions on any person depriving a tenant of the occupation of their property, either as a whole or a part of it. This also extends to prohibiting actions "likely to interfere with the peace or comfort of the tenant or members of his household" where these are intended to get the tenant to give up possession of part or all of the property or to persuade them not to exercise a right.[48] There are defences where there are reasonable grounds for the acts in question or where it

---

[43] In Article 13, 2006 Order.

[44] Articles 54-58, Rent (Northern Ireland) Order 1978.

[45] In s3, Protection From Eviction Act 1977.

[46] *Pirabakaran v Patel & Anor* [2006] EWCA Civ 685.

[47] Article 58, Rent (Northern Ireland) Order 1978.

[48] Article 54, Rent (Northern Ireland) Order 1978.

can be proven that there were reasonable grounds to believe that the tenant was no longer residing in the property concerned. In England it has been held that there is a further defence if a person reasonably believes that someone was not a residential occupier. However, the belief must be reasonable[49] and whether it was or not is a factual matter for the court.[50] While the Northern Ireland legislation is narrower in scope and only protects tenants, as opposed to the wider class of residential occupiers, it seems reasonable to assume that a similar defence would exist in Northern Ireland if it could be shown that there was a reasonable belief that the victim was not a residential tenant.

---

49 *R. v Phekoo* [1981] 1 W.L.R. 1117.

50 *R. v Davidson-Acres* [1980] Crim.L.R. 50.

CHAPTER THREE

REPAIRING OBLIGATIONS, DEFECTIVE PREMISES, AND FITNESS

The Order applied a new regime for repairing obligations, albeit one largely lifted from England and Wales and also brought across the requirement for properties to be fit for human habitation and the legislation relating to defective premises.[51]

Disrepair under the 2006 Order

Northern Ireland has a degree of freedom of contract regarding repairs. This means that the landlord and tenant are free to decide between themselves who will carry out repairs. However, the 2006 Order created a statutory backstop by creating a default set of repairing obligations for landlords[52] if no other obligations are specified.[53] The default obligations are not dissimilar to those that are set out in England.[54] However, the English provisions work by creating a set of provisions that are automatically incorporated in any tenancy contract and cannot be easily contracted out of while Northern Ireland imposes a set of statutory duties that only apply if they have not been contracted out of. However, Northern Ireland adds additional obligations not found in England.

The basic obligations are to keep the structure and exterior in repair and this includes the drains, gutters and downpipes. In addition, the landlord must keep the installations and appliances for sanitation in repair and

[51] Defective Premises (Landlord's Liability) Act (Northern Ireland) 2001.

[52] Article 7, 2006 Order.

[53] Article 6.

[54] s11, Landlord and Tenant Act 1985.

proper working order as well as the installations for gas, water, electricity, space heating and hot water. These are the same as in England. However, Northern Ireland also requires that a landlord keep in repair any appliances for making use of the supply of water, gas or electricity provided by the landlord has provided as part of the tenancy as well as all fixtures, fittings or furnishings provided as a part of the tenancy. In England, the Court of Appeal has held that interior and exterior plasterwork also forms part of the structure of the property and must therefore be kept in repair but does not require paintwork to be kept in good order.[55] However, the Northern Ireland provisions also specify that exterior (but not interior) paintwork must be kept in good order.[56]

The 2006 Order also places obligations on tenants. These are to take "proper care of the premises ... as a good tenant". There is a correlated obligation to carry out repairs of damage caused by the tenant and his associated occupiers. There is also an obligation not to carry out repairs without landlord's consent, which is not to be unreasonably withheld. Finally, there is an obligation on the tenant to keep the interior of the premises in a reasonable state of decoration and the landlord's obligations do not arise to the extent that this applies.

Where a landlord is letting out part only of a property the landlord has an obligation to keep in repair other parts of the property, including parts he does not own, as long as those parts are provided for the use of the tenant. There is an additional obligation to keep parts required for access safe and properly lit.[57] These obligations make more explicit the very nebulously set out requirement in the English legislation which had applied repairing obligations to parts of a property which a landlord had an "estate or interest in".[58]

---

[55] *Grand v Gill* [2011] EWCA Civ 554.

[56] Article 7(2), 2006 Order.

[57] Article 9, 2006 Order.

[58] Section 11(1A) Landlord and Tenant Act 1985.

In England there has been extensive case law on issues of notice,[59] largely because the legislation is totally silent on the issue of notice. Northern Ireland has avoided these issues by simply specifying within the legislation that landlords are not under an obligation to carry out repair works unless they have "actual knowledge (whether because of notice given by the tenant or otherwise) of the need for those works".[60]

However, none of the above applies to the extent that it conflicts with anything written in a tenancy agreement.[61] So landlords and tenants remain free to contract as they please for repairs. That said the statutory regime provides a fairly complete regime for the repair and care of residential properties.

Defective Premises

Prior to the 2006 Order, legislation had been passed quite early in the life of the new Northern Ireland Assembly in respect of defective premises.[62] The 2006 Order applied this to all tenancies created under that Order, so it applies to all residential tenancies which are for less than 50 years or have a rent of more than £1 a year.[63] The old provisions that used to cover this[64] was replaced by this new legislation[65] and does not apply where it does.

---

[59] *Edwards v Kumarasamy* [2016] UKSC 40.

[60] Article 11(2), 2006 Order.

[61] Article 6.

[62] Defective Premises (Landlord's Liability) Act (Northern Ireland) 2001.

[63] Section 3, Defective Premises (Landlord's Liability) Act (Northern Ireland) 2001.

[64] Section 4, Occupiers' Liability Act (Northern Ireland) 1957.

[65] Section 3(3), Defective Premises (Landlord's Liability) Act (Northern Ireland) 2001.

The defective premises legislation largely mirrors the legislation in England and Wales,[66] albeit with some slight updating in terms of adopting a more modern drafting style.

The legislation creates an additional obligation on any landlord who is under an obligation as part of their tenancy to carry out repairs. This additional obligation is a duty to take reasonable care to ensure that people in the property are not injured and do not have their personal possessions damaged due to a defect that they are under an obligation to repair.

The English Court of Appeal has set tight limits on the scope of the legislation. There is no obligation to improve premises or make them safer than they previously were, even if Building Regulations or other standards have changed in the meantime.[67] This is the case even if the work has been done poorly and not following the original plans, provided that nothing has been removed or has broken since the work was done.[68] Nor is there an obligation to carry out a regular programme of inspections or have a policy or process to do so. Although if inspections are carried out they must be done properly.[69]

Fitness Standard

There is a general obligation that privately rented properties must meet a basic standard requiring them to be fit for human habitation. In deciding whether a property is fit the statutory fitness standard must be applied.[70] This specifies that for a property to be fit for human habitation it must:

---

[66] Defective Premises Act 1972.

[67] *Alker v Collingwood Housing Association* [2007] EWCA Civ 343.

[68] *Dodd v Raebarn Estates Ltd* [2017] EWCA Civ 439.

[69] *Rogerson v Bolsover DC* [2019] EWCA Civ 226.

[70] Article 46, Housing (Northern Ireland) Order 1981, inserted by Schedule 5, Housing (Northern Ireland) Order 1992.

- Be structurally stable;
- Be free from serious disrepair;
- Not suffer from dampness prejudicial to the health of the occupants;
- Have adequate provision for lighting, heating and ventilation;
- Have an adequate piped supply of suitable water;
- Have satisfactory facilities in the house for the preparation and cooking of food, including a sink with a satisfactory supply of hot and cold water;
- Have a suitably located water-closet for the exclusive use of the occupants;
- Have a bath or shower and wash-hand basin with a satisfactory supply of hot and cold water again for the occupants exclusive use; and
- Have an effective system for the draining of foul, waste and surface water;

Where the property is a flat, the common areas must also meet a fitness standard requiring them to:

- Be structurally stable;
- Be free from serious disrepair;
- Be free from dampness;
- Have adequate provision for ventilation; and

- Have an effective system for the draining of foul, waste and surface water.

The Department of Communities has indicated that it will interpret the above as requiring reasonably modern kitchens and bathrooms of less than 20 and 30 years age respectively, adequate space and layout of kitchens capable of containing the usual range of modern appliances, a properly located toilet and bathroom which is indoor and is not accessed through a bedroom.[71]

Certain properties are subject to fitness inspections before they can be rented out and they must be certified as fit. The 2006 Order states that any building constructed before 6th November 1956 or based on a conversion of a building constructed before then is subject to inspection.[72] However, it also allows certain properties to be exempted by regulation and the relevant regulations have actually exempted all properties built after 1 January 1945. Even these properties are exempt if they have in the last ten years:[73]

- Had a renovation or HMO grant paid for them;
- Been registered as an HMO; or
- Had a regulated rent certificate issued.

It is necessary to make a formal application for an inspection to achieve certification and this must be done within 28 days of the tenancy being granted.[74] Landlord and tenants can also request a fitness inspection for properties that do not require certification by way of an application.

[71] See www.communities-ni.gov.uk/minimum-fitness-standards.

[72] Article 33, 2006 Order.

[73] Prescribed Dwelling-house Regulations (Northern Ireland) 2007.

[74] Article 33(4), 2006 Order.

There are statutory forms for these purposes as there are for most actions relating to the fitness standard.[75]

If a property is subject to a fitness inspection and has not had one or fails that inspection the property then it becomes subject to rent control. If a property fails then a formal notice of refusal must be served and the landlord may appeal that decision to the county court.[76] If no appeal is lodged or one fails then the Rent Officer will determine an appropriate rent for the property.[77] That rent can be appealed to a Rent Assessment Committee within 14 days of the Rent Officer determining the rent if they do not agree with it.[78] The rules and procedures of the Rent Assessment Committee are set out in regulations.[79] If that appeal is not made or after such an appeal the Rent Officer will register the rent and it will be recorded. Where a fitness inspection is carried out the property is required to be recorded in the rent register. The amount of registered rents are increased periodically by orders and they all rise by a fixed percentage specified in those orders.[80]

If a landlord fails to get a fitness certificate when they should have done then the tenant can recover any sum that they paid which exceeds the sum the Rent Officer determines as the appropriate rent. Therefore a necessary pre-condition to this recovery is for the tenant to apply for a fitness inspection and, potentially, a rent to be registered. The recovery period stretches back to the start of the tenancy and ends when the rent is registered. There is no time limit on the making of such an application until a rent is registered for the property. Once that happens the tenant

---

[75] Found in the Private Tenancies (Forms etc.) Regulations (Northern Ireland) 2007.

[76] Article 37, 2006 Order.

[77] Article 42.

[78] Article 43

[79] Rent Assessment Committees Regulations (Northern Ireland) 2007.

[80] See, for example, Registered Rents (Increase) Order (Northern Ireland) 2019, Registered Rents (Increase) Order (Northern Ireland) 2016.

has two years to seek recovery. The tenant is able to go to court to recover this money but they can also do so by deducting it from their rent.[81]

Where a rent has been registered but the landlord makes the tenant pay more than the proper sum then the tenant has up to two years to recover that money which they can do via the courts or by deduction from their rent.[82]

The Future for the Fitness Standard

The Fitness Standard is an area in which change has been under discussion for some considerable time.[83] It is often seen as a relatively blunt tool which does not assess all aspects of a property and does so in a fairly simplistic fashion. It therefore tends to miss some important areas of fitness altogether[84] while providing excessively interventionist approaches to deal with fairly small issues in other areas. One of the options that has been considered is the adoption of the Housing Health and Safety Rating System (HHSRS) used in England and Wales.[85] This system is a more complex assessment which involves considering a property against a range of 29 hazard profiles and assessing the likelihood of an incident in the ensuing 12 months based on standardised accident data and then considering the seriousness of that putative incident. The advantage of this system is that it provides a (purportedly) objective mechanism of assessing property which deals with the specific hazards and risks in each property on a unique basis. The HHSRS was itself intended to replace the bluntness of previous fitness standards in England and Wales with a more flexible model which would take better account of the different risks in different types of property. In practice, it has been criticised by local authorities as too complex requiring excessive resources

---

[81] Article 52, 2006 Order.

[82] Article 51.

[83] See www.communities-ni.gov.uk/publications/review-housing-fitness-standard.

[84] Adequate space and security, for example.

[85] Found in Part 1, Housing Act 2004.

in daily use making it unworkable and it is poorly understood by landlords and tenants. The Upper Tribunal has also highlighted the complexity of the regime[86] and questioned how objective it actually is as it still relies on significant amounts of individual judgement.[87] In fact, the HHSRS in England is currently being reviewed and is potentially subject to significant change.[88] It might be a little odd therefore for the Northern Ireland government to advance quickly to introduce it into Northern Ireland as it stands.

---

86 *Bristol City Council v Aldford Two LLP* [2011] UKUT 130.

87 *Bolton Metropolitan Borough Council v Patel* [2010] UKUT 334.

88 See www.gov.uk/government/publications/housing-health-and-safety-rating-system-outcomes-of-the-scoping-review.

CHAPTER FOUR

LEASES AND LICENCES – WHAT CONSTITUTES A RESIDENTIAL TENANCY?

All of the major UK jurisdictions have enduring questions as to whether a residential occupation constitutes a licence or a tenancy. In England & Wales the main deciding point is based on a decision of the House of Lords Judicial Committee.[89] This case simplified the position in England and Wales by holding that "circumstances are that residential accommodation is offered and accepted with exclusive possession for a term at a rent, the result is a tenancy." In fact, the position is even easier in England and Wales because the Court of Appeal has since concluded that the suggestion by the House of Lords that a tenancy is for a "term at a rent" is not an absolute statement rent is also not an absolute requirement in that a rent can be zero or a nominal figure and a tenancy can still exist.[90] England has therefore tended towards a tight focus on the issue of exclusivity of possession and this has become the essence of a tenancy. Northern Ireland has in general also adopted the reasoning of the House of Lords and so in most cases a person occupying a property for residential purposes and having exclusive possession will be a tenant.

However, the position in Northern Ireland is slightly altered by a statute common to Ireland and Northern Ireland, Deasy's Act.[91] This act was created partly to allow for the protection of agents who let out lands on

[89] *Street v Mountford* [1985] UKHL 4.

[90] *Ashburn Anstalt v Arnold* [1989] Ch. 1, CA.

[91] More properly called the Landlord and Tenant Law Amendment (Ireland) Act 1860.

behalf of landowners in England. The key point of the Act therefore was to allow the relationship of landlord and tenant to be created between parties even where the landlord did not hold the reversionary interest in the land because they were an agent and not the landowner.[92] This creates the somewhat unique position in Ireland and Northern Ireland that a lease can be created between parties even where the landlord is not in fact an owner of the land and has no estate or interest in it. The relationship of landlord and tenant is therefore entirely one that subsists based on an actual or implied contract.[93] The same statute also requires that tenancies of longer than 12 months be created in writing.[94] However, commentators suggest that the fact that a tenancy subsists orally does not in itself prevent a tenancy arising. Where a tenancy is created without the full requirement of writing being met then the general view is that a periodic tenancy from rental period to rental period will be created. This will usually be for less than 12 months and so will not violate the Act.

The Court of Appeal has held that Deasy's Act is partly there to enable tenancies to arise where the Common Law would not otherwise permit this to happen. It is not intended to be dictatorial on the point. So, if the parties had no intention to create a tenancy then Deasy's Act will not normally override that wish.[95] Therefore, the fact that a rent was being paid and exclusive possession of land given does not automatically create a tenancy where one would not otherwise arise. However, the issue of intention is one that remains uncertain in Northern Ireland. As the law has developed in England the intention of the parties is one that the Court has construed on an objective basis. It has done this to avoid being taken in by sham agreements that seek to misstate the position and to avoid procedural devices. It is uncertain what position should apply in Northern Ireland. Commentary has suggested that the same principle

[92] Alan Dowling, "New landlords: problems and solutions: Part 2", NILQ 59(4): pp 349-78.

[93] Section 3, Landlord and Tenant Law Amendment (Ireland) Act 1860.

[94] Section 4, Landlord and Tenant Law Amendment (Ireland) Act 1860.

[95] *Todd v Unwin* [1994] NIJB 230.

should apply in Northern Ireland.[96] However, the focus in Deasy's Act on a contractual relationship based on "express or implied" contractual intention of the parties suggests that intention is of greater import in the creation of the relationship. The cases that deal with this issue in Northern Ireland[97] pre-date the leading House of Lords decision[98] and so the point is not settled in Northern Ireland. The key difference between Northern Ireland and England is that in England the question of the existence of a tenancy is one of land law and so the Courts are free to take a view of intention that is more unique to that sphere and seeks to protect tenants who have made a home based on their understanding of intention and focusing on exclusivity of occupation. However, Deasy's Act has moved the question of the existence of a tenancy into the sphere of contract law and a more restrictive view of intention then applies. Therefore, far from the relatively expansive view of intention adopted in England which seeks to create tenancies even where the landlord is not themselves in possession of one[99] the position in both Ireland and Northern Ireland has been restricted more strongly by Deasy's Act. It has been argued, with some force, that the test of exclusive occupation in Northern Ireland is much looser than that in England and the intention of the parties must be looked at more carefully, and given greater respect, when deciding whether a tenancy has been formed rather than the narrow focus on exclusive possession more common in England.[100]

The issue of rent has also arisen. This is a concern as s3 requires that a tenancy must have a "consideration of … rent". However, that does not mean that a rent cannot be zero or be variable such that it might from

[96] Catherine Turner et al, The Law of Property in Northern Ireland (Belfast: Colourpoint, 2014), pp. 160-1.

[97] *Northern Ireland Housing Executive v McCann* [1979] NI 39 (HC); *Northern Ireland Housing Executive v Duffin* [1985] NI 210 (HC).

[98] *Street v Mountford* [1985] UKHL 4.

[99] *Bruton v London and Quadrant Housing Trust* [1999] UKHL 26.

[100] Mark Hayward, "Exclusive possession or the intention of the parties? The relation of landlord and tenant in Northern Ireland" NILQ 68(2): pp 203-23.

time to time be zero and the courts have not made clear whether this constitutes a tenancy or not. In fact the Court of Appeal has been fairly generous in its interpretation of rent, following old Irish case law. There is no requirement that a payment specified under a contract need be periodical in nature to be rent.[101] Further the Court of Appeal has been generous in implying the existence of a rent from fairly flimsy evidence including a payment of £1 in a draft lease appended to an option agreement. However, in the same decision, the Court of Appeal intentionally broke from the English case law and from commentary on Northern Ireland property law[102] in holding that Deasy's Act absolutely requires a payment of rent for a tenancy to exist in Northern Ireland and that without such a sum the relationship of landlord and tenant could not exist. Any occupancy granted without a rent reserved will therefore be a contractual licence only.[103]

Accordingly, a tenancy in Northern Ireland exists where exclusive possession is intentionally granted to an individual by a person who is held out as their landlord and a rent is paid by the tenant for the privilege of that occupation. If that tenancy is for more than 12 months it must be reduced to writing otherwise a licence will be formed.

---

[101] *Crane v Naughten* [1912] IR 318.

[102] See, for example, Turner et al, *The Law of Property in Northern Ireland* (Belfast: Colourpoint, 2014), pp. 160-1.

[103] *Northern Ireland Renewables Limited v Carey (Harry)* [2016] NICA 30.

CHAPTER FIVE

TENANT FEES

All the main UK jurisdictions now have legislation restricting or prohibiting the charging of fees to tenants. In the cases of England[104] and Wales[105] this legislation was introduced relatively recently. In Scotland most such fees had been banned for some time[106] but the ban was clarified and extended more recently[107] as the original prohibition had been forgotten and was being widely flouted. In NI there has also been a historic prohibition which had been similarly forgotten until its more recent revival.[108] The NI prohibition was on asking a tenant to pay any commission or any part of it due from a landlord to an agent, which includes any other fee, charge, or expense. This applies specifically to any disposal of land or to rent reviews or renewals or extensions of the tenancy agreement. In two recent decisions the County Court has held that these restrictions should be construed relatively widely as including the tenant paying any money that the landlord has had to pay the agent for the letting of the property and specifically cover work done by an agent that if the agent had not done the Landlord would have to do themselves.[109]

However, the legislation does not appear to restrict the charging of fees to prospective applicants for referencing costs and the like if these are not part of the fee being charged to the landlord for the professional services of the agent. All fees are fact specific and so it would be open in any case

[104] Tenant Fees Act 2019.

[105] Renting Homes (Fees Etc) (Wales) Act 2019.

[106] Rent (Scotland) Act 1984.

[107] Private Rented Housing (Scotland) Act 2011.

[108] Commission on Disposal of Land (NI) Order 1986.

[109] *Loughran v Piney Rentals Ltd* [2017] NICty 2.

to argue that a fee charged was not for the letting or renewal of the property, but a general expense charged by an agent which was not specifically for their professional services in procuring the letting. An attempt to get the County Court to make a wider declaration stating that all such fees were unlawful where an agent was engaged on a landlord's business has been rejected.[110] However, the *Piney* case makes it hard to say that a fee charged by an agent does not fall within the scope of the ban because of the reasoning that brings a fee into scope where it is charged for something the agent is doing that the landlord would otherwise have to do themselves. By that reasoning, the limits can only be escaped if they relate to a fee for work done that is specific to an agent's role as agent and would not be something that a landlord would otherwise have to do for themselves. This would probably mean that permissible fees were limited to being things that the agent had contracted with the tenant to do for the tenant's benefit.

In addition, these restrictions do not prohibit a landlord charging additional fees on their own account as long as they are not doing so in order to remunerate or help remunerate an agent. They also do not limit the charging of fees for the provision of a reference at the end of a tenancy unlike the equivalent English legislation. There is also no restriction on liquidated damages clauses which charge a fixed fee for specific breaches of the tenancy agreement. These are also prohibited in England while in Wales the Welsh Ministers have the power to prohibit them if they wish.

There are proposals[111] to review the tenant fee restrictions in Northern Ireland to introduce new legislation which mimics that in England.

---

[110] *Loughran v F5 Property Ltd* 16/084351.

[111] Department for Communities, Private Rented Sector in Northern Ireland – Proposals for Change, Consultation Document January 2017.

CHAPTER SIX

RATING

Northern Ireland does not have Council Tax. Instead properties in NI are liable for rates based on their assessed capital value. This system is essentially the same as the system which existed in England & Wales before the introduction of the Poll Tax/Community Charge which then became Council Tax.

The rating system, much like the Council Tax system in England and Wales, is at times wilfully confusing. The basic obligation is to pay rates in respect of a hereditament. This is defined as being a "property which is, or would fall to be shown as a separate item in the" rating list.[112] This very open-ended definition essentially allows a vast degree of latitude to Land and Property Services in the Department of Finance[113] which maintains the rating list.

The liability to pay rates normally falls on the person occupying a property.[114] However, in respect of tenanted properties it is possible for the liability to fall on the owner of the property concerned, usually the landlord. This is decided by way of a methodology largely based on the capital value of the property. In summary, the owner is liable to pay rates rather than the occupier if the property has a capital value of less than £150,000 or if it is let as an HMO.[115] Just as occupiers are allowed to claim rate rebates for unoccupied property, so are landlords.

---

[112] Article 2, Rates (Northern Ireland) Order 1977.

[113] www.finance-ni.gov.uk/topics/property-valuation/domestic-valuation.

[114] Article 18.

[115] Article 20.

It is also open to a landlord to make an agreement with the Department of Finance whereby he agrees to pay the rates, not receive any rebate for empty property, and to pay promptly in advance. Doing so allows a rebate of up to 10% of the rateable value to be obtained.[116]

The Department of Finance is authorised to send a notice to an owner requiring them to set out the names and addresses of persons occupying the property or properties that they are paying the rates for and setting out the periods for which the property or properties have been vacant.[117] Equally, the Department may serve a notice on the occupier or on a person paying rent for a property asking them to set out:

- The nature of the occupier or rent payers interest in the property;
- The date on which they acquired that interest;
- The rent payable in respect of the property and the dates on which it falls due;
- The amount of rent currently due;
- The date on which he began to occupy the property; and
- The name and address of the owner of the property.[118]

The landlord is permitted to require the tenant to pay the rates as part of the terms of the tenancy agreement or to bundle them into the rent. Tenants are not allowed to deduct rates from their rent unless it is in reimbursement of rates they have paid because their landlord has broken an agreement to pay those rates for them. Where rates are payable by the

[116] Article 21.

[117] Article 22.

[118] Article 26, 2006 Order.

tenant on the basis of a clause in the tenancy agreement then failure to make that payment can be treated as rent arrears.

Normally, unless it is clearly stated otherwise the rates are assumed to be bundled into the rent. If the rates for the property move up or down the rent is automatically moved up or down by the same amount.[119]

In many ways the system is open to abuse. By making landlords liable for rates and then encouraging them to pass that liability on there is a risk that landlords will load additional administration or other costs into the figure the tenant is ultimately charged. Therefore the process that at one level makes the process easier for the bodies asked with collecting the rates, and largely eliminates the need to chase tenants who have left for unpaid sums also places those tenants further at the mercy of unscrupulous landlords who might be tempted to use rates as a justification for excessive rents.

119 Schedule 8.

CHAPTER SEVEN

SAFETY REGULATIONS

The safety requirements in relation to private tenancies in Northern Ireland are very similar to or the same as those in England and Wales although they are again starting to slip behind those being operated in England[120] and those that are shortly to come into effect in Wales.[121]

Gas

As with all other parts of the UK, Northern Ireland has regulations about the safety of gas appliances.[122] One regulation applies specifically to landlords and, in general terms, requires them to obtain an annual gas safety check. Responsibility for ensuring compliance with the Gas Safety Regulations in Northern Ireland falls with the Health and Safety Executive of Northern Ireland.[123] They have contracted with Gas Safe Register[124] to operate the necessary registration scheme for appropriate individuals who are permitted to do work on gas appliances. In fact, the gas regulations as regards landlords are almost exactly the same as those in England & Wales.

The obligation to obtain a gas safety certificate is imposed on a landlord of any residential tenancy which is for less than seven years or which is periodic or which has arisen out of such a tenancy. The obligation does

---

[120] In the Electrical Safety Standards in the Private Rented Sector (England) Regulations 2020.

[121] In the Renting Homes (Wales) Act 2016.

[122] Gas Safety (Installation and Use) Regulations (Northern Ireland) 2004.

[123] www.hseni.gov.uk.

[124] www.gassaferegister.co.uk.

not apply in respect of any tenancy longer than seven years. As is common in these situations any part of the tenancy which pre-dates the grant of the tenancy is not counted within the seven years and neither is any part of a tenancy that falls after a landlord's break clause. So, a tenancy for eight years which allows for a landlord to break the tenancy at four years is a four-year tenancy for these purposes. If a tenancy is for less than seven years but contains an option to renew for the tenant which would take the aggregate length of the tenancy over seven years then it will be a tenancy of more than seven years for the purpose of gas safety obligations. If the property is let on a residential licence then the licensor is always obliged under the gas safety regulations unless the licensor is himself a tenant with a tenancy of less than seven years in which case the obligation moves up the chain. So, a flat owned by a freeholder which was leased for 99 years to A and then sub-let for 2 years to B and occupied by C under a licence would find A being liable for the provision of a gas safety certificate as that would be the first person moving up the chain with a tenancy of more than seven years.

Landlords have four specific obligations under the gas safety regulations. First and foremost they are obliged to ensure that the gas fitting (which includes the pipework, appliances and flues) is maintained in a safe condition.[125] Second they must ensure that only properly authorised individuals carry out work on those gas fittings.[126] Thirdly, there is an obligation to procure a safety check of the gas fitting by an authorised person and that check must be repeated every twelve months.[127] Fourthly a copy of that inspection report must be provided to the tenant before they occupy the premises and within 28 days of each renewal of the report.[128]

[125] Regulation 36(2).

[126] Regulation 36(4).

[127] Regulation 36(3).

[128] Regulation 36(5).

A safety report must be repeated strictly within 12 months of the previous report. There is no grace period and if the check is carried out early then the extra time between the date of the check and the ending of the original certification period is lost. There tends, therefore, to be a degree of brinkmanship in the operation of gas safety certifications in practice with landlords leaving them to the very last minute. Where a gas fitting is a new installation then the installation certificate suffices as the safety certificate for the first 12 months. Those safety records must also be kept for two years from the date of the check and a tenant is entitled to ask to see that record at any time.[129]

The safety record must be provided to a new tenant prior to them moving in. This is frequently done incorrectly in practice and it is common for landlords to mix up the obligation to supply a new tenant with a copy of the gas safety record and the obligation to supply a copy of the annual renewal record within 28 days such that many landlords believe that the obligation is to supply a copy of the certificate within 28 days of the tenancy commencing. There is a slight relaxation of this process for properties where no gas appliances are found in the area occupied by the tenant or where the tenant is not occupying the premises for more than 28 days. In these cases, a copy of the record can be displayed in a prominent position in the premises and a note placed on it stating that a tenant can request their own copy.[130]

The regulations are prescriptive about the things that a gas safety record must contain. At a minimum these are:[131]

- the date on which the check occurred;
- the address of the premises at which the check was done;

[129] Regulation 36(5).

[130] Regulation 36(7).

[131] Regulation 36(3)(c).

- the name and address of the landlord or agent;
- a description and the location of each item checked;
- any defects identified and remedial action taken;
- confirmation that the check undertaken complies with the minimum requirements set out in the gas safety regulations;
- the name and signature of the individual carrying out the check; and
- the registration number for the person or organisation carrying out the check with the Gas Safe Register.

The Court of Appeal in England and Wales recently had cause to consider the gas safety legislation. While it was primarily concerned with the interaction between gas safety records and notice to end tenancies it did make clear that a gas safety record which did not record the information required correctly was invalid. So, a record which misstated the date on which the inspection was carried out due to a clerical error was not a valid record.[132] The regulations do however allow that the signature does not have to be on the copy of the record supplied to the tenant as long as a copy with the signature on it is retained and the tenant in advised that they are able to inspect that copy at will.[133]

A landlord cannot contract with or agree with a tenant to get them to manage or carry out the safety checks themselves. In fact, the regulations state that nothing done by a lawful occupier can be taken into account in assessing whether a landlord has complied with his obligations. However, the exception to this is the issue of access.[134] If an occupier denies access

132 *Trecarrell House Ltd v Rouncefield* [2020] EWCA Civ 760.

133 Regulation 36(8).

134 Regulation 36(10).

for the carrying out of a check then this can be taken into account in deciding whether or not a landlord has complied with his or her obligations. The Northern Ireland Health and Safety Executive state that they expect landlords to use all reasonable measures to obtain access. This includes a clear written notice seeking access and giving the reasons why that access is required. They also suggest a log is kept of efforts to obtain access which suggest that more than one effort is expected. The English HSE has guidance that states that landlords must make several efforts to obtain access using different modes of communication in order to satisfy their obligations and that at least one of these must allow the tenant to propose or choose form a selection of appointment times as well as explaining the safety benefits to the occupier of a check.[135] While HSE Northern Ireland has no equivalent statement the wording of their guidance with the suggestion of a log being kept indicates that they would expect a similar approach.[136]

Furniture and Furnishings

The Furniture & Furnishings (Fire) (Safety) Regulations 1988 apply in Northern Irealnd in the same manner that they do in the rest of the UK. Therefore, all furnishings that contain foam and which were made after 1950 should have the relevant safety label attached.

---

[135] www.hse.gov.uk/gas/domestic/faqlandlord.htm.

[136] www.hseni.gov.uk/publications/landlord-duties-relation-gas.

CHAPTER EIGHT

DISCRIMINATION

Discrimination legislation in Northern Ireland has a history distinct from that in the rest of the United Kingdom, largely due to the different discrimination problems that arise in Northern Ireland. Northern Ireland has tended to lag behind the rest of the United Kingdom in the implementation of discrimination legislation and has focused more on ensuring equality between the two primary religious groupings than on dealing with other types of discrimination. Anti-Discrimination legislation began in 1970 with the introduction of the Equal Pay Act which established the principle of equal pay between men and women. More substantial legislation was passed in 1976 creating the Equal Opportunities Commission for Northern Ireland and making discrimination on the grounds of gender unlawful.[137] At a similar time legislation was introduced to prevent discrimination in employment on the grounds of religion.[138] There was then something of a hiatus until 1997 when legislation was introduced to bar racial discrimination.[139] Much of the original push for legislation originated in the workplace and the need to ensure that women and religious minorities were not unfairly treated. More recently the legislation has sought to move beyond that to ensure fair treatment across society for vulnerable groups. In more recent times Northern Ireland position has passed legislation equivalent to that

[137] Sex Discrimination (Northern Ireland) Order 1976.

[138] Fair Employment (Northern Ireland) Act 1976, later replaced by the Fair Employment and Treatment (Northern Ireland) Order 1998.

[139] Race Relations (Northern Ireland) Order 1997.

in England and Wales.[140] This means that discrimination in relation to property will be unlawful under any of the following grounds:

- Race
- Sex
- Disability
- Sexual Orientation
- Belief

While England and Wales have moved on again and have wider protected categories the conceptual bases of the legislation are similar and the law has tended to be treated as being much the same within those protected categories.

---

140 Disability Discrimination Act 1995 and the Equality Act (Sexual Orientation) Regulations (Northern Ireland) 2006.

CHAPTER NINE

ENERGY PERFORMANCE

Just as with the rest of the UK, Northern Ireland is required to comply with European Directives on energy efficiency.[141] Initially the government was being somewhat relaxed about compliance in Northern Ireland until the European Commission threatened legal proceedings for failure to comply. As a result, the government rushed through legislation in 2008.[142] These bear a strong similarity to the similarity named regulations for England and Wales. These were updated in 2014[143] in part to comply with an updated EU directive.[144]

The requirement is that an Energy Performance Certificate is obtained for a property which is to be rented out and that this must be shown freely to any prospective tenant at the earliest opportunity. In all cases it must be made available before the tenancy is granted and a copy must be given to the tenant at that stage.[145] The copy does not have to be a physical one and an electronic copy can be given or made available so an

141 Specifically, Directive 2002/91/EC of the European Parliament and of the Council of 16 December 2002 on the energy performance of buildings.

142 Energy Performance of Buildings (Certificates and Inspections) Regulations (Northern Ireland) 2008.

143 By the Energy Performance of Buildings (Certificates and Inspections) (Amendment) Regulations (Northern Ireland) 2014.

144 Directive 2010/31/EU of the European Parliament and of the Council of 19 May 2010 on the energy performance of buildings.

145 Regulation 5.

emailed version of the certificate or a link to a website where the certificate is displayed would both be acceptable.[146]

In all key respects the EPC system is the same in Northern Ireland as it is in England and Wales and Domestic Energy Inspectors accredited in one area can operate in the other, and vice versa.

Enforcement is through local authorities by way of civil penalty[147] which is fixed at £200.[148] The local authority must give notice of the intended penalty and then they must allow not less than 28 days for responses. A final notice is then served and this can be appealed to the county court.[149]

146 Regulation 9.

147 Regulation 33.

148 Regulation 35.

149 Regulation 37.

CHAPTER TEN

LANDLORD REGISTRATION

Landlord registration has been spreading across the various UK jurisdiction. Scotland has had landlord registration since late 2005.[150] The perceived success of that regime has led other parts of the United Kingdom to consider their own regimes. Wales passed legislation to allow for landlord registration in 2014,[151] although it did not come into force until 2016. Northern Ireland created its own regime at approximately the same time as Wales,[152] but it came into force much more quickly, in February 2014. There was a slight amendment to the regime in 2016,[153] but it has remained largely unaltered since its introduction.

While all three of the major devolved jurisdictions have a landlord registration scheme, the regimes in the three of them are quite different and there is not a lot of comparison between them. The Northern Ireland regime is very light touch in its operation and is genuinely little more than a register of landlords as opposed to the regime in Wales, for example, which has a code of conduct and a requirement for landlords to take a prescribed training course. The NI government is empowered to appoint someone to run the scheme and has appointed the Landlord Registration Scheme to run the registration scheme in NI.

---

[150] Antisocial Behaviour etc. (Scotland) Act 2004.

[151] Housing (Wales) Act 2014.

[152] Landlord Registration Scheme Regulations (Northern Ireland) 2014 authorised by s65A Private Tenancies (NI) Order 2006. Provision inserted by the Housing (Amendment) Act (NI) 2011.

[153] Landlord Registration Scheme (Amendment) Regulations (Northern Ireland) 2016.

Registration is required immediately prior to a new tenancy commencing so it is not acceptable to commence the tenancy and then register later.[154] There are no grace periods in the regulations. The requirement to register is specified in the regulation as requiring that a "landlord letting a dwelling- house must register with the registrar". However, the exact meaning of the words used is important. The regulations do not define a dwelling house or the concept of letting and the definition of landlord is pretty vague. The enabling legislation defines a "dwelling-house" as including a part of a house but says little more than this. The definitions of "landlord" and "let" include sub tenancies falling under an original tenancy.[155] Therefore, a landlord letting a flat is still required to register even though they are also a tenant under a superior landlord who owns the building that the flat is within. However, it appears that a property which was genuinely let under a licence would not require registration as it would not involve a landlord and tenant and neither would a let for a holiday as it would not be a dwelling-house.

An application must include:[156]

- The landlord's:
    - full name;
    - date of birth;
    - address;
    - a correspondence address if that is different. If the landlord is based outside NI then the correspondence address must be in NI;

154 Regulation 4.

155 See Article 2, Private Tenancies (NI) Order 2006.

156 Schedule 1.

    - email address;
    - telephone contact details including mobile telephone details.

- If the landlord is a company, the company registration number;
- For each property being let by that landlord:
    - the address with postcode;
    - the date the house was built; and
    - the name and contact details of any joint owners;
- the name, address and contact number of any agent acting for the landlord;
- If the property or properties are HMOs then:
    - The HMO certificate number for each property that is an HMO; and
    - The address of each HMO.

The registration fee is specified in the regulations as £70 for each landlord, or £80 if the application is made on paper.[157] That fee covers every property that the landlord owns. However, as with other schemes a distinction is drawn between property ownership in a landlord's personal capacity and through a company. Landlords with HMO licences are exempt from the registration fee, but not from the requirement to register. Although the regulations are unclear on the point, in practice where properties are owned jointly only one fee is charged and one person can register on behalf of all the joint owners.

---

[157] Schedule 3.

A registration is valid for three years. At that point it is necessary to re-register, updating any altered information and to pay a further fee, which is currently the same amount as the previous fee. There is no grace period in the legislation for re-registration and so the obligation is to register prior to the original registration running out.

The publicly visible register will not show all the information submitted to the scheme.[158] It will only display the name and registration number of each registered landlord and their full contact details of any agent acting for them. The full register data can be disclosed to other local and national bodies to allow for the matters such as the collection of rates, the administration and enforcement of HMO and property standards obligations and for the management of state benefits.[159]

Agents occupy a slightly odd place under the registration regime. The regulations require a registering landlord to specify any person acting on their behalf in relation to the letting or management of the property. The details of that agent will also be published in the publicly visible component of the register. However, it is less than clear whether agents need to register. The guidance page for landlords using agents does not explicitly state that agents are exempt from registration and deals more with whether agents are responsible for situations where a landlord they are working for does not register.[160] The guidance states that agents are not liable and indeed the regulations are clear that it is the landlord who must register. Naturally, if an agent has agreed with a landlord that they will manage the registration process for that landlord there may be a contractual duty owed to register and failing to perform the agreed obligation may also be negligent but there is no liability under the registration regulations. There is no mechanism for agents to register themselves in their own right. However, this is not really what the

[158] Schedule 2

[159] Regulation 9, inserted by regulation 3 of the Landlord Registration Scheme (Amendment) Regulations (Northern Ireland) 2016

[160] https://www.nidirect.gov.uk/articles/information-landlords-who-use-agents

regulations say. The definition of a landlord in the registration regulations specifically states that a landlord "includes a person acting on behalf of the landlord in relation to a tenancy".[161] This suggests that agents are expected to fulfil every obligation that a landlord is expected to fulfil in terms of registration. The obligation to register falls on "a landlord letting a dwelling house"[162] and so if the interpretation provision is to be accepted they should fall equally on a "*person acting on behalf of* a landlord letting a dwelling-house". So, it seems that the regulations do say an agent is required to register. Given that no mechanism to do so exists it would be hugely unreasonable to prosecute an agent in this circumstance and no doubt this has prevent. But if a mechanism was later created to allow for direct tenant enforcement as has happened in England, where tenants can seek to recover rent paid for some offences regardless of whether there has been a prosecution,[163] then this point might create an unexpected problem for agents. In relation to tenancy deposit protection in England the High Court has held that the similar form or words stating that a landlord included a person acting on their behalf was sufficient[164] to fix an agent with liability for the penalty of three times the deposit in a case where the landlord had not protected it properly in accordance with the relevant legislation.[165]

The regime also requires that a landlord provides a tenant with his registration number in any correspondence that "relates to the discharge of his functions as a landlord".[166] This does not appear to require placing it in the tenancy agreement or into any statutory forms but it must be listed in letters sent to the tenant.

---

[161] Regulation 2.

[162] Regulation 3.

[163] Housing and Planning Act 2016.

[164] *Draycott v Hannells*

[165] ss212 & 214, Housing Act 2004.

[166] Regulation 8.

Unlike in other parts of the UK the enforcement regime does not allow for any form of direct tenant enforcement. There are three possible offences under the legislation. Providing false information in a registration application, letting a property without being registered, and failing to provide the tenant with the registration number as required. Enforcement is by way of prosecution with a maximum fine of £2,500 for providing false information or letting a property without being registered or £500 for the offence of not providing the tenant with the registration number.[167] There is also the power for district councils to issue a fixed penalty as an alternative to prosecution.

[167] S65A(4), Private Tenancies Order.

CHAPTER ELEVEN

HOUSES IN MULTIPLE OCCUPATION

As with the rest of the UK, Northern Ireland has its own detailed regime which applies to Houses in Multiple Occupation (HMOs).[168] This reflects the increased risks associated with this type of accommodation and the greater prevalence of poor standards in such accommodation. It also reflects the fact that the HMO sector is estimated as comprising 14,000 properties, a significant fraction of the whole.[169] Originally this regime was operated by the North Ireland Housing Executive, but that scheme has been removed and replaced with a new scheme operated by district councils. The substantial legislative importance given to this area is reflected in this text by the space allotted to it.

Many aspects of the HMO regime in Northern Ireland owe a great deal to similar legislation and its operation in England and Wales.[170] However, Northern Ireland has learned from some of the problems that have been experienced in England and Wales, closing some of the loopholes and fixing problems which have plagued the English legislation. Unfortunately, as is to be expected with such a complex regime, others remain and new ones have been created.

Unfortunately, as it has in England and Wales, the HMO regime in Northern Ireland has also spawned a plethora of subsidiary Statutory Instruments to give effect to its requirements. In part this was due to

---

[168] Houses in Multiple Occupation Act (Northern Ireland) 2016.

[169] *The Private Rented Sector in Northern Ireland: Profile and Key Issues*, Norther Ireland Assembly Research and Library Services, Briefing Note 50/09, para. 9.

[170] Housing Act 2004.

Northern Ireland partially aping the design of the legislation in England as well as an effort being made to keep a degree of flexibility in a complex regime. This has made it a bit of a minefield to navigate and substantially increased the complexity of the regime.

A property is an HMO if it is a building or any part of one which is:

1. it is living accommodation;
2. it is occupied by 3 or more persons;
3. those persons occupy the property as their only or main residence;
4. those persons form more than two households, and
5. rents are payable or other consideration is to be provided in respect of the occupation by at least one of those persons of the living accommodation.[171]

Living Accommodation

Living accommodation is specifically defined in the HMO Regulations. In order to be seen as living accommodation a property must:

- Be, or be able to be, occupied as a separate dwelling;
- Be in single ownership;
- Have the occupiers sharing a toilet, cooking facilities, or personal washing facilities.[172]

It is worth noting here that the specific terms of the occupation are not relevant. So a tenancy is likely to be living accommodation but so is a licence. So the HMO regime cannot be avoided by not granting a

---

[171] Section 1, Houses in Multiple Occupation Act (Northern Ireland) 2016.

[172] Section 2.

tenancy. Likewise, the threshold for occupation of a property as a separate dwelling is relatively low. It is not a "term of art" and should be given its plain English meaning. So, a single room is capable of being occupied as a separate dwelling and the test is ultimately whether or not it is a place in which an occupier reasonably makes his or her home.[173]

The definition of a household is also clearly specified. In practice, it means that a household is composed entirely of people who share a direct family relationship. This is slightly artificial as it takes no account of how people live but merely of their blood relationships to each other. So, three friends who share a house, cooking and eating together and sharing all bills will be seen as three households whereas two sisters with their husbands who live entirely separately in one house, cooking separately and rarely speaking to each other would be seen as one household.

The family relationship includes couples, parents, grandparents, children, grandchildren, brothers, sisters, uncles, aunts, nephews or nieces. Unlike in England and Wales it does not include cousins.[174] It also includes step and half-blood relations who are to be counted as full relations. A couple includes those who are married or civil partners or who live as if they were married.

Just as in England and Wales there is an inherent flaw in the definition in that there is no central point in the group, it is a chain of relationships rather than a web fixed around an individual. Therefore, if I live with my uncle and his nephew (my cousin) and the partner of that nephew and their children and the maternal grandparent of those children we will all be one household provided the chain of relationships prescribed by the legislation is maintained. If my uncle were to move out the chain would be broken and we would become two households (one being me, the other being my cousin and his family). so, in the first example if there is also one unrelated person living in the house as a lodger then it will be two households (one being the lodger, the other being everyone else) and

---

173 *Uratemp Ventures v Collins* [2001] UKHL 43.

174 Section 88, Houses in Multiple Occupation Act (Northern Ireland) 2016.

so not an HMO. In the second example it will be three households and the property would be an HMO.

As well as family members someone will be part of the same household if they are engaged to provide care or domestic help and their contract of employment requires them to reside in the premises.[175] So an *au pair* would be part of the household of her employer for the purposes of the HMO regime. In addition, so are members of that employee's family. So an *au pair* who had a child would find that they were both members of their employers family for the purposes of the HMO regime.[176]

One of the useful ways that the Northern Ireland legislation has learned from problems found in England relates to disputes over the number of households in a property. In England there is no good way of resolving such disputes expect through the council seeking to prosecute the landlord and then having to show that individuals are not related, which is not simple. In Northern Ireland, by contrast, a district council has the option of serving a notice, called a household notice, on any or all of the owner, property manager, or occupiers stating that they believe that there are more than two households present in the property and seeking evidence to the contrary. Such a notice can be served where the council reasonably believes that there are more than two households and must specify the reasons why the council believes this. The notice must specify a period of 28 days to respond giving evidence as to why the council's belief is incorrect. If no evidence is provided or insufficient evidence provided to reasonably make the council change its view then it is able to serve a final household notice and at that point the occupation of the property will be deemed as consisting of more than two households. There is then a right of appeal to the county court. This effectively reversed the burden of proof and puts the onus on the occupiers and property owner to show that the property is not an HMO. For landlords it is important to consider the issue if groups are presenting to them claiming to be one or two households with complex relationships. It

[175] Section 4(2), Houses in Multiple Occupation Act (Northern Ireland) 2016.

[176] Section 4(3).

would be worth getting them to set out their relationships in full to one another and for every occupant to sign this. This would then provide reasonable evidence of the landlord's belief in the number of households and may also prove protective if the tenants later assert that there are more than two households to a district council.

Exceptions

There are some specified exemptions to the regime[177] and properties that fall into these will not be HMOs. That means that no aspect of the HMO regime will apply to these properties. Properties will not be HMOs where:

- They are managed or in the control of a governmental body or a registered social service care provider;

- They are regulated by some other statutory provision and which is set out in regulations made by the Northern Ireland government. Currently, no regulations have been made so no property falls within this exception;

- They are occupied mainly or entirely by students in full-time further or higher education and the educational establishment is managing the property or it is purpose-built managed student accommodation for more than 15 full time students run by a private company. In addition, the educational establishment must be expressly named in the relevant regulations[178] or it, or a private company managing student accommodation, must be a signatory to either the Universities UK or the Accreditation Network/Unipol standards for managing student accommodation;

[177] Schedule 1, Houses in Multiple Occupation Act (Northern Ireland) 2016.

[178] The Houses in Multiple Occupation (Specified Educational Establishments) Regulations (Northern Ireland) 2019.

- They are mainly occupied by a religious community whose principal occupation is prayer, contemplation, education or the relief of suffering;

- They are owned by the Crown and occupied only by members of the armed forces along with members of their household;

- They are a prison, a young offenders centre, a juvenile justice centre or a remand centre; or

- They are occupied only by someone who owns a freehold or leasehold interest in the property which is for more than 21 years along with members of that person's household and their lodgers. It is open to the government to limit the number of lodgers by way of regulations but no such regulations have been made and so the number of lodger is theoretically unlimited.

Licensing

Every HMO as set out above must be licensed by the relevant district council.[179] A licence will specify key facts about the property and its ownership but must also set out the maximum number of people who are permitted to occupy it and any other conditions which the relevant district council reasonably consider appropriate.[180] Licences are obtained by application. Belfast city council administers the HMO application process for all district councils in NI and all applications are made through them.[181] However, they simply process the applications and actual decisions are made by each individual district council. District councils are organised into clusters with a single council leading each

[179] Section 7, Houses in Multiple Occupation Act (Northern Ireland) 2016.

[180] Section 4(3).

[181] nihmo.belfastcity.gov.uk.

cluster and provided support and advice to the local authorities within that cluster.

An application for an HMO licence must be in writing and in such form as the council may specify.[182] In fact, as Belfast Council runs the scheme for every District Council the format is actually specified by Belfast for all councils. The legislation states that an application must include:

- the address of the property for which a licence is being sought;
- the name and address of the owner if the owner is an individual. If it is a corporate entity or partnership then the name of the entity and its main office along with the names and addresses of all the directors or partners;
- the details of any proposed managing agent
- the name and address of any person or entity who co-owns the freehold, holds a leasehold interest or has a mortgage or other charge over the property;
- the proposed maximum number of people who will occupy the HMO.

The government may also make regulations requiring other information to be given although no such regulations have been made. District Councils may also seek further information as part of the application process. It is worth noting that in England the wording of the legislation is different and states that the ability of local authorities to require further information on licence applications is "subject to any regulations made" by the relevant Secretary of State. This has led to local authorities having their application processes challenged and overturned by the court.[183]

[182] Schedule 2, para 1.

[183] *R(Gaskin) v Richmond Upon Thames London Borough Council & Anor* [2017] EWHC 3234 (Admin).

The Northern Ireland legislation does not follow this route and allows for regulations to specify further information sought and then also allows for district councils to specify yet more information they seek in addition. So, the restriction that is found in England and Wales by which local authorities cannot seek information that is beyond that which is specified by regulations does not appear to apply in Northern Ireland.

Advertising of application in local papers

Uniquely, any applicant for an HMO licence in Northern Ireland must advertise the fact of that application in at least one newspaper which circulates in the area in which the HMO is found within 7 days of submission of the application.[184] A copy must also be given to the HMO application body. That advert must include:

- The name of the person applying for a licence;
- The property that an HMO licence is being sought for;
- The number of occupants that the licence application is for;
- Which district council is deciding the application; and
- A statement that there is a right to make representations about that application.[185]

If there is no advert published and provided then the HMO application will not be processed. In fact, no processing will commence until a copy of the advert has been provided. There is a limited power for a licence applicant to be excepted from this obligation if the council is satisfied

[184] Regulation 2, Houses in Multiple Occupation (Notice of Application) Regulations (Northern Ireland) 2019.

[185] Regulation 3.

that requiring an advert would "jeopardise the safety or welfare of any persons or the security of any premises".[186]

There is a slight oddness in this requirement. Local newspapers are disappearing across the UK or, more commonly, are moving to online publication. As such, they can be said to circulate everywhere. That being the case it becomes increasingly hard to be clear which newspaper the advert should be placed in. A similar problem has plagued local authorities in England who are obliged to advertise their local HMO licensing schemes in two local newspapers. Increasingly, they are unable to find two such publications to advertise in.

As well as the obligation on a licence applicant to advertise their application the council must also place a notification of the application on their website and must also notify any occupier of a neighbouring property of the application.[187] Anyone who wishes to respond to such a notice has 28 days to make a written representation.[188]

Application Process

Where a council is in receipt of a valid application it also has notification requirements.[189] The council must publish a notice of the application for an HMO licence, in a similar form to that which the applicant must publish in a local newspaper, on its website. It must also serve a copy of that notice on any identified occupier of neighbouring land to the proposed HMO.[190] The council must also send a copy of the licence application to:

---

[186] Regulation 5.

[187] Regulation 4.

[188] Regulation 6.

[189] Schedule 2, Houses in Multiple Occupation Act (Northern Ireland) 2016.

[190] Regulation 4, Houses in Multiple Occupation (Notice of Application) Regulations (Northern Ireland) 2019.

- the Chief Constable;
- the Department for Social Development
- the Northern Ireland Fire and Rescue Service Board,
- the Northern Ireland Housing Executive, and
- Any other authorities that have been appointed by regulations. Currently there are none.

Representations in response to notice of an application for an HMO licence must be made in writing and must set out the name and address of the person making the representation. These representations must be received by the council within 28 days of with the date on which the council published the notice of the HMO application on its website.

Fees

An HMO application must also be accompanied by a fee. The legislation allows for regulation to be made specifying maximum fees and the calculation mechanism for those fees. A maximum sum for those fees can be set by regulations and this has been done,[191] with the fee capped at £45 for each occupier of the HMO per annum. In fact, at the time of writing the current fee for an HMO licence application is actually set at less than the maximum, at £37 per person per annum. When calculating the fee the district council is required to take into account the cost of running the scheme and all the additional obligations that the council is required to carry out under the HMO legislation. This is somewhat more generous than the equivalent regime in England which more strictly limits local authorities to their costs. However, there is some question as to whether this charging regime complies with the EU Services Directive

[191] Regulation 2, Houses in Multiple Occupation (Fees) Regulations (Northern Ireland) 2019.

and the UK regulations which derive from it.[192] These regulations state that a fee for an "authorisation scheme" which an HMO licensing regime is must be reasonable and proportionate to the cost of the procedures and formalities under the scheme and must not exceed the cost of those procedures and formalities.[193] In England, the High Court has held, following ECJ decision making,[194] that an application fee for an HMO licence in England must only be for the application itself and should not include additional cost elements.[195] Therefore, at the very least, the parts of the current HMO fee that are not specifically for the application itself and are earmarked for general scheme operation and enforcement should be refundable to landlords who are not successful in their licence application. Currently, there is no mechanism for this within the Northern Ireland charging regime. It would appear therefore that the fee structure being utilised across Northern Ireland is not fully in accordance with EU law and the domestic law which brings it into effect and so a number of landlords who have had licences refused might be entitled to seek refunds of part of their fee.

Other fees

The legislation also specifically allows further fees to be charged for the provision of a certified copy of an entry on the HMO register.[196] As with the application fee regulations can specify a maximum sum and this has

[192] Provision of Services Regulations 2009. Post-Brexit these are amended by the Provision of Services (Amendment etc.) (EU Exit) Regulations 2018 but the main provisions are unchanged.

[193] Regulation 18(4).

[194] Hemming (Judgment) [2016] EUECJ C-316/15.

[195] *R(Gaskin) v Richmond Upon Thames London Borough Council & Anor* [2018] EWHC 1996 (Admin).

[196] Section 62(12), Houses in Multiple Occupation Act (Northern Ireland) 2016.

been done capping the fee at £15.[197] The fee charged for the copy by Belfast Council is the maximum.

Determining an application

In determining an application the relevant district council must satisfy itself of a number of things. These are that:

- Allowing the property to become an HMO would not create a breach of the planning permissions for that property;
- the owner of the property and anyone managing it are fit and proper;
- The management arrangements for the property are satisfactory;
- Allowing the HMO would not cause there to be too many HMOs in the area;
- The property is fit for human habitation;
- The property is suitable for occupation by the specified number of people or can be made suitable by appropriate licence conditions

The determination must be completed within 3 months of the application being made. An application can be made to the court to extend this. If the council fails to make a determination in the appropriate time then then the application is deemed granted automatically in the terms it was applied for.[198]

197 Regulation 3, Houses in Multiple Occupation (Fees) Regulations (Northern Ireland) 2019.

198 Schedule 2, para 12, Houses in Multiple Occupation Act (Northern Ireland) 2016.

Approval

If the local authority is minded to grant a licence then a notice must be served on the applicant and on all relevant persons stating that it is their intention to grant the licence, giving the reasons, giving the terms of the proposed licence and giving at least 14 days to make representations. At the end of that period a final decision must be made and a notice served giving that decision, enclosing a copy of the licence granted, give reasons for any differences between the granted licence and the licence applied for, and give the date the decision was made. The decision notice must be served within seven days of the decision date.

The licence once granted can last for a maximum of five years or a minimum of six months. However, between those two figures the council is free to set any time length it likes. However, in England the Upper Tribunal has been clear that there must be a clear and principled policy reason for setting time limits and that these cannot be set on an arbitrary basis without good reasons which actually reflect the objectives of the licensing process.[199]

Refusal

If a licence is refused on the basis of lack of planning consent then the local authority must serve a notice on the applicant within 28 days of the decision to refuse stating that the decision has been made to refuse a licence, giving the reasons for that decision, and giving information about the right to re-apply.[200] If the refusal is for any reason other than planning then a notice must be served on the applicant and on all relevant persons stating that it is their intention to refuse the licence, giving the reasons and giving at least 14 days to make representations. On the basis of those representations the final determination is made and a final decision

[199] *Waltham Forest v Khan* [2017] UKUT 153, *Waltham Forest v Reid* [2017] UKUT 396.

[200] Schedule 2, para 6.

notice must be sent with the reasons and with copies of any written representations made.

Limits after refusal

If a licence application is refused, other than where the refusal is based on the basis that the there is no planning consent for the HMO, then there is an automatic bar on any further application for an HMO for that property for the period of a year. If the licence is refused on the basis that any person involved in the application is not a fit and proper person then that person is deemed not to be a fit and proper person for the purpose of any HMO application for the same period of one year. This is not a total bar as a council can consider a licence application during the one-year period if they are of the view that there has been a change of circumstances which merits this. If the licence was refused due to not having appropriate planning consent only then the applicant can seek planning consent or a certificate of lawfulness. If they then re-apply for an HMO licence within 28 days of obtaining that permission or certificate then the HMO licence application fee is waived.[201]

Variations

The legislation provides for a range of powers to vary licences[202] and sets out a process for that variation.[203] A council can vary a licence at their own behest or on the request of the licence holder or anyone else who has an obligation imposed on them by the licence. The permissible variations are:

- Changing the number of people allowed to occupy the property;
- Changing the managing agent for the property;

201 Schedule 2, para 7, Houses in Multiple Occupation Act (Northern Ireland) 2016.

202 Section 22.

203 Schedule 4.

- Changing any of the conditions on the licence.

If the local authority is asked to or is deciding to vary the licence or if it has been asked to vary the licence and is refusing to do so then the local authority must start by serving a notice on:

- the property owner;
- if different, anyone applying for a licence variation;
- the Chief Constable;
- the Department for Social Development
- the Northern Ireland Fire and Rescue Service Board,
- the Northern Ireland Housing Executive, and
- Any other authorities that have been appointed by regulations. Currently there are none.

This notice must specify whether the council is proposing to vary or refuse to vary the licence, set out what the variation is if the proposal is to vary the licence, and then give the reasons for the proposed variation or refusal to vary. Finally, the notice must give a period of time to submit written representations on the proposal. A council can choose to hold a hearing based on either the original request to vary or on any submission it receives.[204] If they intend to do so then they must give at least seven days notice of that hearing and serve a notice giving the date, time and location of the hearing on:

- the owner and any other person applying for a variation;

[204] Schedule 4(3), Houses in Multiple Occupation Act (Northern Ireland) 2016.

- any person who has or will have a condition imposed on them that is affected or created by the proposed variation;

- anyone else that the council considers appropriate.

Before making a final decision the council must consider all written representations and any made at a hearing. Once the decision is made the council must then serve a final notice of its decision on all of the people set out above who should have had a copy of the original proposal notice. That notice must be served within seven days of the decision being made. That final notice must specify the date of the decision, the decision made, the reasons for that decision, and enclose a copy of any varied HMO licence. If the variation was made in response to an application and the decision is to vary the licence but in a manner different from that applied for then the reasons for the different variation must also be given.

Interestingly, Belfast Council charges a fee for a change of owner or managing agent and a fee for the addition of further occupiers. These are part of the variation process. However, the legislation does not specify any power to seek a fee for variations and the original licence fee should in fact cover these changes as the legislation expresses that the fee may include "all costs incurred by the council in carrying out its functions under this Act". In other words, all additional work, such as the cost of variations should be incorporated within the basic application fee. There is no power provided under the legislation to make any additional charge for work involved in a variation of a licence and, indeed, the wording of the legislation specifically suggests that such a fee is not permitted as it should be incorporated in the original fee for the HMO licence itself. In England the lower tribunals have held that the charging of additional fees for HMO licence variations is unlawful and most councils have stopped making these charges as a result.[205] However, it is not a point tested in more senior courts and these lower tribunal decisions would carry limited weight in Norther Ireland. However, the reality is that the legislation

[205] *Crompton v Oxford City Council*, CAM/38UC/HMV/2013/0006-7.

does not authorise the additional fee and there is a case for refusing to pay it and then seeking to judicially review or otherwise appeal the refusal to process the licence variation requested or, alternatively, taking a claim against the council for charging a fee unlawfully.

No variation takes effect until the window for an appeal has passed or any appeal is determined, including allowing time to appeal to a higher court.

Revocation

A council can also choose to revoke a licence.[206] However, a council can only revoke a licence for specific statutorily defined reasons. These are that:

- the HMOs owner or managing agent is not a fit and proper person;
- the management arrangements are unsatisfactory;
- the HMO is not fit for human habitation;
- the HMO is not suitable for occupation regardless of the number of persons the occupancy is limited to and cannot be made suitable by adding or changing the licence conditions;
- the owner, managing agent, or any other person who an HMO licence imposes an obligation on has committed a serious breach of a licence condition; or
- there have been two or more breaches of licence conditions.

[206] Section 23, Houses in Multiple Occupation Act (Northern Ireland) 2016.

- The process for a renovation is set out in the statute[207] and is the same as that for a variation as set out above.

As with a variation, no revocation takes effect until the window for an appeal has passed or any appeal is determined, including allowing time to appeal to a higher court.

Surrender of a licence

Unlike in England and Wales there is a specific power to surrender the licence.[208] This allows the licence holder to give notice to the council that they wish to surrender the licence. The council can set out the format of such a notice but at the time of writing no council appears to have done so. However, the legislation gives no scope for the council to refuse such a surrender. The legislation gives no date or means of calculating the date on which such a surrender takes effect. Presumably this means that it takes effect when the notice is received and processed by the relevant council.

Sale of an HMO

There are specific provisions as to what happens when a licensed HMO is sold.[209] It appears again that Northern Ireland has learned lessons from, or at least anticipated, problems in England and Wales as the regime there is entirely silent on the issue, leaving the Upper Tribunal to interpret the situation and conclude that licences in those jurisdictions automatically terminate on sale of the relevant property.[210] In Northern Ireland HMO licences do not automatically terminate and they can be transferred between property owners subject to specific rules. The new owner must apply for a new HMO licence prior to the date of transfer of ownership. Provided that they do so then the old licence held by the

---

207 Schedule 4.

208 Section 27.

209 Section 28.

210 *Taylor v Mina An Ltd* [2019] UKUT 249 (LC).

previous owner will temporarily be treated as being held by the new owner of the property from the date of transfer of property ownership. If the new owner's licence application is granted then the old licence will cease and the new licence will take over. If the new owner's HMO licence application is refused, then the old licence will terminate one month after the final date on which an appeal against that refusal could be made. These provisions are in fact wider than I am giving them credit for as they do not apply solely to sale but to any change of ownership. So, if a property were transferred as part of insolvency or divorce proceedings or by way of inheritance, this provision allows the licence to continue seamlessly as well.

Death of Licence Holder

If a licence holder dies, the HMO licence does not immediately terminate. It effectively follows the property as it is deemed to be held by the personal representatives of the deceased owner as from the date of death.[211] This lasts for a period of three months from the date of death at which point the licence terminates. It is open to the personal representatives to ask the district council, within the initial three-month period, for the licence to be extended further. The council can do so, and there is no limit on the length of time that they can do so for, provided they consider that it is "reasonable to do so for the purpose of winding up" the estate of the deceased owner.[212] The council is required to serve a notice of its decision in response to an extension request on the personal representatives. Notwithstanding the extension created by this section of the Act the licence can terminate earlier than the extension period if the council revokes it using its powers to do so, or if it is surrendered by the personal representatives, or if the ownership is transferred to someone else.

211 Section 29, Houses in Multiple Occupation Act (Northern Ireland) 2016.

212 Section 29(2).

Joint licence holders

Where more than one person owns a property which is an HMO then an HMO licence can be held by any one of those individuals solely but it can also be held by a number of them jointly.[213] Where there are obligations in relation to HMOs they fall on the owner or owners who actually hold an HMO licence except that the various offences relating to not having a licence at all are offences that all of the owners commit jointly. Joint owners can sell their interests to one another or to third parties and the outgoing owner can then apply to be removed from any HMO licence. Councils cannot refuse such a request. Where new joint owners come on board they can apply to be added to a licence held by the existing owner.

Temporary Exemption

Where an individual finds themselves in control of an HMO and does not wish to be they can avoid the licensing regime by seeking a Temporary Exemption Notice (TEN) provided they then proceed diligently to change the occupancy of the property such that it rapidly ceases to be an HMO. This might happen where a tenant has breached the agreement and brought other people into a property, where a property has been purchased and unexpected occupiers found, or where a property has been inherited with occupiers in place. The implication from the wording is that a TEN is intended for situations where the owner has inadvertently found themselves in possession of an HMO. However, in England the Tribunals have been more generous in permitting TENs to be granted to allow landlords to simply elect not to run an HMO, however those case were generally found early in the existence of the HMO licensing regime when it was still a new process. There were reports when HMO licensing was introduced in Northern Ireland that landlords were seeking to remove tenants, often unlawfully,

[213] Section 69.

to avoid properties becoming licensable.[214] A TEN would certainly be preferable to an unlawful eviction.

In these cases, they can apply to the relevant District Council for a Temporary Exemption Notice (TEN).[215] Any application for a TEN must as part of that application set out the particular steps the owner is proposing to take to ensure that the property ceases to be an HMO and also include an undertaking to carry out those same steps. Provided that the council considers the proposed steps will have the effect of stepping the property being an HMO and that the owner actually intends to carry them out then the council can choose to issue a TEN. The council must serve on the owner a notice of its decision to issue or decline to issue a TEN and must also serve the same notice on the occupants of the HMO. A TEN has the effect that the HMO is not required to be licensed for the three-month period for which it lasts. The owner may further apply for an extension of the TEN for a further three months.[216] The legislation specifically states that an extension can only be given where there are "special circumstances" which implies that an extension requires a better justification than an initial TEN. Only one such extension is allowed. As with an original TEN the council must serve a notice on the owner and the occupants of the HMO as to whether it will grant or refuse an extension.

A TEN may include conditions set by the council requiring the owner to carry out various works on the property to improve the safety or security of the occupants during the TEN period.[217] Those works must be specified in the TEN notice along with the dates by which they must be carried out. The notice may also specify the manner in which the works are carried out. The legislation is not clear as to whether an extension can

[214] www.housingrights.org.uk/news/evictions-unintended-consequence-hmo-enforcement.

[215] Section 15, Houses in Multiple Occupation Act (Northern Ireland) 2016.

[216] Section 16.

[217] Section 17, Houses in Multiple Occupation Act (Northern Ireland) 2016.

include further conditions not set out in the original TEN. However, as an extension request seeks nothing more than an extension of the original TEN, the assumption must be that no further requirements can be added.

Where works are required to a building which is listed as being of special architectural or historic interest, is subject to a preservation notice, to is in a conservation area then the council cannot require those works without first consulting the relevant government department. A council may also extend the deadline for completing works on the request of the owner or occupants, or of its own volition to such later date as the council considers suitable. However, the council may only extend a deadline if satisfactory progress has been made in the works, a good explanation has been given for unsatisfactory progress or a written undertaking has been given by the owner to complete the works by a suitable date. If an extension is given then the council must serve notice of that extension on the person who asked for it and on the owner and their managing agent (if any).[218]

Where the council has added requirements to the TEN then if the owner is not complying with them it may choose to revoke the TEN. If it does so it must serve notice of the decision to do so on the owner and occupants. The owner can appeal that revocation and so it does not come into effect until the last possible date to appeal has passed or the appeal process is exhausted.

Agents

Agents are not required to be registered under the HMO legislation or more generally. However, in applying for an HMO licence a landlord must specify any managing agent that is operating the property for them. This managing agent must be named on the ultimate HMO licence. For the purpose of the HMO legislation an agent is defined as anyone who:

218 Schedule 3, Part 1.

- receives the rent or similar periodic payment from people living in the property. This is subject to an exception that an agent who is simply receiving the first rent payment only (ie a let only agent who sets up a tenancy but has nothing further to do with it) is not an agent for this legislation;
- arranges any repairs or refurbishment for the property; or
- sends or receives communications to the occupiers or council about the property.[219]

A person is also a managing agent if they do anything else to assist in the management of the HMO.[220]

Using an agent who is not named on a licence is an offence as is being that agent without having a reasonable excuse. This definition creates a slight problem in that the addition of the segment suggesting that anyone who assists in management is also an agent is a little wide. In principle this could encompass the spouse of a landlord who assists in organising repairs or a plumber who arranges for an electrician to accompany him on a job to attend to some other work that needs doing.

Standards

The HMO legislation contains two parts linked to standards of the property, both with supplemental regulations. The first of these relates to the amount of space available for the occupants, especially in their individual rooms and the second relates to the general standard of the accommodation.

Space standards fall within the general definition of overcrowding. An HMO is overcrowded[221] if it fails to meet wither the room standard or

[219] In section 88(1), Houses in Multiple Occupation Act (Northern Ireland) 2016.

[220] Section 33(3)(b).

[221] Section 41.

the space standard. The room standard[222] simply states that an HMO is overcrowded if the number of people sleeping in it as compared to the number of rooms available for sleeping would require a person over the age of 13 to sleep in the same room as another person of the opposite sex over the age of 13 (unless they are a couple) or in the same room as a couple.

The space standard[223] is essentially an update of a similar standard found within similar legislation in England and Wales.[224] The room standard works on a soaring mechanism. The number of people living in the HMO are scored. Persons under the age of one are not counted and children between one and eleven count as a half person. The HMO itself is then given a notional maximum number of occupiers which is calculated by measuring the floor space of each room that is useable as sleeping accommodation and then following the table given to assign notional number of occupiers to it. When measuring the floor space regard must also be had to supplementary regulations[225] which set out how to measure the floor area. These state that the floor area must be measured at floor level, must ignore the effects of skirting and must discount areas that have a ceiling height of less than 1.525m. There are also exclusion where chimney breasts intrude into the space and for the small gap behind the entry door. Ultimately, once the notional number of occupiers is calculated, then this number must exceed the actual number of occupiers, otherwise the property will be overcrowded.

The space standard is not a standard which sets out how big each room must be. It is an aggregate standard which sets out how much space there needs to be as a whole in the property. In that sense, it is not a terribly useful measurement mechanism for an HMO as it tends to assume that

[222] Section 42.

[223] Section 43.

[224] Section 326, Housing Act 1985.

[225] Houses in Multiple Occupation (Space Standard) Regulations (Northern Ireland) 2019.

a smaller room can be made up for by having a much larger room next door. This is true of a normal family home where space can be traded off between individuals but it is rather less realistic in an HMO where individual occupants may have little connection with one another and are unlike to agree to share their personal space. A similar problem characterised the space standards in England and for this reason a new standard was introduce for HMOs specifying a minimum room size.[226] It should be borne in mind that the existence of a minimum space standard does not prevent a local authority using the licensing process to block the use of rooms which they consider to be excessively small.

The other set of standards are those required to be met when considering the suitability of an HMO for a specified number of people.[227] These are set out in some detail in regulations.[228] These regulations set out minimum standards for:

- Lighting, both natural and artificial;
- Ventilation;
- Hearting, hot water, and sanitation;
- Sinks, showers and toilets;
- Food storage and preparation;
- Kitchen sinks;
- Fire safety signage;

[226] In the Licensing of Houses in Multiple Occupation (Mandatory Conditions of Licences) (England) Regulations 2018.

[227] Section 13, Houses in Multiple Occupation Act (Northern Ireland) 2016.

[228] Houses in Multiple Occupation (Living Accommodation Standard) Regulations (Northern Ireland) 2019.

- External and interior walls;
- Safety equipment; and
- Rubbish disposal.

The regulations are quite prescriptive. Unlike the English equivalent regulations[229] they set out specific sizes for refrigerators and worktops, for example. The Act also requires that the council considers the location of the property and the number and type of people occupying it, their safety and security, and the possibility of public nuisance. The council is not permitted to consider any property as suitable if it fails to meet these minimum standards but they can still consider a property unsuitable even if it does meet these standards. However, the Act does not permit local authorities to set their own standards. In England, the Upper Tribunal has held that local authorities can have guidance as to what they consider suitable but that as the English legislation does not empower them to set standards they can only use that guidance as guidance and not as a standard by which they can objectively judge properties.[230] While English UT cases are not binding in Northern Ireland the underlying rationale for the decision is valid in the context of the structure of the Northern Ireland legislation. The Supreme Court has also held in considering standards that it is valid for a local authority to apply different considerations to property occupied by students.[231] So local authorities can, and should, consider the type of occupant and apply the relevant standards differently.

Code of Practice

The Act provides that the Northern Ireland government may make regulations setting out a code of practice that must be followed in the

[229] Schedule 3 of the Licensing and Management of Houses in Multiple Occupation and Other Houses (Miscellaneous Provisions) (England) Regulations 2006.

[230] *Clark v Manchester City Council* [2015] UKUT 129 (LC).

[231] *Nottingham City Council v Parr & Anor* [2018] UKSC 51.

management of HMOs.[232] Such regulations have indeed been made.[233] These do nothing more than identify a code of practice published by the Northern Ireland government that must be followed.[234] The Act sets out things that may appear in a code but it is not prescriptive. It also allows for the code to be modified or withdrawn by regulations at any point. However, in approving a code or a change to it the Act requires the relevant department to hold a consultation on the new code or modification with people who manage and people who live in HMOs or appropriate representatives of them. A general consultation on a range of matters involving HMOs along with the proposed code of practice was held in November 2018.[235]

Failure to abide by a code of practice is not in itself an offence and does not make a person liable to civil proceedings either. So, no landlord can be prosecuted by the local authority or have a claim made by his or her tenants on the basis of failing to properly apply the code of practice. However, it is a relevant matter when considering whether a person is fit and proper.

Much of the approved code of practice restates existing obligations under the law as it stands. However, there are some noteworthy additions.

The code of practice itself is required to be displayed in the HMO premises. A notice is also required setting out the name, address and telephone number of the person or persons who manage the property and making explicit that they are the manager. If they also collect the rent

---

[232] Section 63, Houses in Multiple Occupation Act (Northern Ireland) 2016.

[233] Houses in Multiple Occupation (Code of Practice) Regulations (Northern Ireland) 2019.

[234] Currently The Houses in Multiple Occupation Act (Northern Ireland) 2016: Code of Practice for the Management of Houses in Multiple Occupation available at https://www.belfastcity.gov.uk/documents/nihmo/code-of-practice-for-management-of-houses-in-multi.

[235] Available at https://www.communities-ni.gov.uk/publications/houses-multiple-occupation-hmo-subordinate-regulations.

that must also be clearly set out. There is also an obligation to take reasonable measures to ensure that this information remains displayed so it will need to be robustly placed and renewed as necessary.

The code also requires that all electrical appliances receive a portable appliance test (PAT) every five years and that all firefighting alarms and equipment are maintained and tested regularly. The code also brings in the relevant guidance on HMO fire safety and effectively makes complying with this guide part of the code as well.[236]

The code is quite interesting in that it actually replicates large parts of the regulations in England and Wales, often using the same wording, that specify how HMOs must be managed.[237] The key difference between England and Wales and Northern Ireland is that the regulations in England and Wales have full statutory force and failing to comply with them is a strict liability offence which can, and has, led to prosecution. In Northern Ireland the code is not something that has direct enforcement attached to it and so failing to comply with it does not lead to immediate prosecution. That said, many of the obligations in the code are set out elsewhere in statute and so those statutes often provide enforcement powers even if the code itself does not.

Reasonable excuse

Certain offences within the Act include a defence of reasonable excuse. This is a common defence in criminal law in the United Kingdom, especially in relation to strictly liability offences. The courts have been fairly clear as to what categories of defence might constitute a reasonable excuse. In general, the bar is high and a reasonable excuse cannot be used to undermine the fact that the relevant law making institution elected to make the particular offence one of strict liability in order to keep everyone on their toes. However, rather unusually the Northern Ireland Assembly

---

[236] The HMO Fire Safety Guide, available at https://www.nifrs.org/wp-content/uploads/2019/09/HMO-Fire-Safety-Guide-V1.pdf.

[237] Management of Houses in Multiple Occupation (England) Regulations 2006.

has chosen to set out things that might constitute a reasonable excuse for a breach of the HMO legislation.[238] This is almost unique. The list is not exhaustive and so the general approach to reasonable excuse must be assumed to remain intact. The legislation however further allows for a reasonable excuse defence to be made out where an offence is being committed but the landlord is not able to remedy it without breaching the terms of a tenancy agreement that was in existence prior to the offence being committed. This is a little unusual. In England and Wales, a far harder line is taken and a landlord that is so unwise as to draft a tenancy agreement or place themselves in a position in which they cannot resolve an HMO offence without breaching the terms of the tenancy will simply face the consequences of their actions. This section is also potentially rife with opportunities for breaching the legislation. For example, a reasonable excuse is a permitted defence for breaching a licence condition on an HMO licence. If a landlord were to write their tenancy in such a way that they had committed to the tenants to breach that condition then they would presumably have a reasonable excuse defence to any ensuing prosecution.

Information requests

District Councils have powers to seek information to assist them in carrying out anything they are required to do under the HMO legislation. They can also seek information to establish if an offence has been committed.[239]

A council may also serve a formal notice on any person who:

- Holds or has applied to hold an HMO licence for a HMO;
- Is or has applied to be the managing agent for a HMO;

[238] Section 34, Houses in Multiple Occupation Act (Northern Ireland) 2016.

[239] Section 70.

- Is the owner or occupier of the premises or appears to be;
- Receives rent, whether directly or indirectly, for an HMO or appears to do so.

A notice must give the person it is sent to at least 21 days to respond. There are two types of notice available under the legislation. A notice can either require written information to be produced[240] or it can require the production of documents specified in the notice.[241] There are specific limits on these powers. A notice requiring documents to be produced cannot require any document to be produced which is subject to legal professional privilege.[242] Equally, information provided in response to a notice cannot be used in evidence, in other words there is a privilege against self-incrimination. The exception to this is where information is provided and the person providing it later tries to advance a defence in court that is inconsistent with the information provided in response to the notice.[243]

A council may also serve a notice on a range of other persons involved in a property seeking information. This includes government departments, the operators of landlord registration and tenancy deposit schemes, letting and managing agents and other persons connected with a property.[244]

Failure to provide information in response to a notice is an offence which is punishable by a fine of up to £500.[245] A local authority employee who discloses information derived from a notice without lawful authority also

[240] Section 71, Houses in Multiple Occupation Act (Northern Ireland) 2016.

[241] Section 72.

[242] Section 72(4).

[243] Section 71(4)-(6).

[244] Section 73.

[245] Section 75.

commits an offence and can be fined or imprisoned for up to two years, or both.[246]

Powers of entry

Council officers may give 24 hours written notice to the owner of a property as well as to the occupiers of the property in order to enter the premises to inspect. This inspection is to decide whether:

- The property is a HMO;
- To grant, vary or revoke an HMO licence;
- To carry out any of their other roles under the HMO legislation.[247]

It is also possible to apply to a lay magistrate for a warrant to enter a property if the council is investigating whether an offence has been committed under the HMO legislation and to ask for access would undermine the purpose of seeking entry in the first place.[248]

Obstructing a lawful inspection is an offence unless there is a reasonable excuse to do so.[249]

---

[246] Section 76.

[247] Section 78.

[248] Section 79.

[249] Section 80.

CHAPTER TWELVE

FIXED PENALTIES

Fixed penalties are available as an enforcement option across a range of housing matters in NI. There are two regimes operating under different legislation but which are functionally similar. One under the Private Tenancies Order covering a range of offences across different regulatory elements[250] and another for breaches of the HMO rules.[251]

If the council wants to issue a fixed penalty they must have reasonable belief that an offence has been committed. Notably this is a lower standard than that required in England,[252] which requires a prosecutor to believe that an offence has been committed beyond reasonable doubt. The council begins the process by an officer authorised in writing by the council for the purpose of enforcement of the registration regime giving a notice setting out:

- Reasonable information about the offence and the circumstances in which it is alleged to have been committed;

- The fixed penalty that is being proposed for the offence. This must not exceed £500 for a false information or letting without a registration offence or £100 for the failure to provide the registration number offence;

---

[250] s68A, Private Tenancies Order, inserted by s8, Housing (Amendment) Act (NI) 2011.

[251] Ss 64-6, Houses in Multiple Occupation Act (Northern Ireland) 2016.

[252] Housing Act 2004, s249A.

- A period in which to pay, which must be at least 14 days, during which a prosecution will not be commenced; and
- the person to whom and the address at which the fixed penalty may be paid.

It is important to note that fixed penalties have a maximum. There is no suggestion in the legislation that they should always be that sum although given that the sums are relatively low it is likely that they will trend towards that figure. However, a District Council should be considering the level of the penalty and how it sets it. It should also be noted that there is nothing in the legislation which prevents a District Council from seeking multiple penalties where multiple offences have been committed. The normal common law limits on offences would need to be observed here. So it would be inappropriate to charge a landlord for five separate offences of not putting their landlord registration number on a letter to a tenant. These are one offence which has been committed several times. However, it might be appropriate to charge a landlord with failing or register as a landlord and also with failing to put the registration number on a letter. In that case it would be equally appropriate to levy two separate fixed penalties, one in respect of each offence. When setting the penalty sum, however, a consideration would need to be given to the issue of totality. So the total penalty would need to reflect the seriousness of the overall offending and not simply be the sum of all the constituent penalties. Therefore where a District Council is levying multiple penalties they should set a penalty for each offence but then add the total penalty up and consider whether it is a fair reflection of the seriousness of the offending or should be reduced and then go back and adjust the various constituent penalties downwards to reach that revised figure.

If the penalty is paid within the set period then a prosecution may not be commenced. If it is not paid then prosecution can go ahead. In any dispute over whether or not the fixed penalty was paid and the date on which it was paid then a certificate signed by the clerk of the council giving that information is evidence of that fact.[253] The statute does not state that a certificate is "conclusive" evidence of the fact however so it can be disproved. However, the evidence would need to be strong.

The clear advantage to a District Council of a fixed penalty regime is that they are able to retain the money for their own use. However, a District Council is limited in its use of funds derived from penalties. A District Council can only use funds from penalties to fulfil functions required of them under the Private Tenancies Order or such other matters as are set out in secondary legislation from time to time. At the time of writing no other use for these funds has been prescribed. This approach mirrors that used for fixed penalties for housing matters in England which only permits the funds derived to be used for housing related purposes.[254]

There is no fixed guidance from central government as to how District Council's should apply their penalty powers. However, individual District Councils have in fact written their own policies with statements as to how they will deal with this. Guidance in England for local authorities has suggested that they should:

- Set out how they will decide what cases are to be prosecuted and which will attract penalties;
- Set out how they will exercise their discretion to enforce or not to; and
- Set out the factors which will be used to calculate the penalty.

In England the guidance for Crown Prosecutors and guidance from the sentencing council on levels of harm and culpability has been used profitably. However, this is of less value in Northern Ireland as Northern

253 Section 68A(9) Private Tenancies (NI) Order.

254 See the Rent Repayment Orders and Financial Penalties (Amounts Recovered) (England) Regulations 2017.

Ireland sentencing guidance is more specific and has no guidance on harm and culpability. However, the guidance on totality is relevant in cases where multiple offences have been committed and a number of fines are being considered.

The fixed penalty regime in NI is different from the regime in England which requires a prosecutor to choose a penalty or prosecution at the outset and then proceed with that choice throughout.[255] It in fact mirrors the scheme in Wales including mirroring the statutory language. The Welsh structure also allows a prosecutor to offer a penalty as an alternative to prosecution but to proceed to prosecute if the penalty is not paid.[256] At the time of writing there are no cases from Wales which would assist with the interpretation of the provisions in Northern Ireland.

[255] See s 249A, Housing Act 2004 for example

[256] See s29, Housing (Wales) Act 2014.

CHAPTER THIRTEEN

APPEALS

Any decision made by a local authority under the HMO regime is potentially subject to an appeal to the County Court.[257] Likewise, decisions made by local authorities under the 2006 Order are also subject to appeal. These include any civil penalty notice[258] and decisions around landlord registration[259] and fitness.[260]

Appeals can only be made but a person who was required to be served with a copy of the relevant notice that is being appealed.

Statement of reasons

For decisions under the HMO regime, and certainly any decision which can be appealed to the county court, a council is required to give a formal notice when making the decision.[261] This notice must always include a statement setting out the right to seek a statement of the reasons for the decision that is set out in the notice or the decision to serve the notice depending on the specific type of notice being served. The notice must also include a statement setting out the right to appeal the notice. The statement of reasons must be asked for within seven days of the service of the notice and the council is required to provide a statement within 14 days of receipt of the request. As an alternative the council can avoid the request process by simply providing a statement of reasons along with the

---

[257] Section 67(2), Houses in Multiple Occupation Act (Northern Ireland) 2016.

[258] Article 68A, 2006 Order.

[259] Article 65A.

[260] Article 37.

[261] Section 68, Houses in Multiple Occupation Act (Northern Ireland) 2016.

relevant notice. If they do so then there is no requirement for a notice to contain any information about the right to request a statement of reasons and there is no requirement for a council to provide a further such statement.[262] There remains a requirement to include information about the right to appeal.

Appeal time limits

The time limits on appeals under the HMO legislation are quite tight. Ordinarily appeals must be made within 28 days of the service of a notice or, where the appeal is against a decision, 28 days of the date of service of the notice of that decision. If a statement of the reasons for a decision being made has been sought then the time limit on appeal is seven days after the statement of reasons has been sought if that is later. In principle this should not happen in that a statement of reasons must be sought within 7 days of service of the notice and the statement is then required to be provided within fourteen days.[263] The time limit on an appeal is then seven days after that statement of reasons has been served which again amounts to 28 days from the service of the original notice. However, the legislation is clearly allowing for the possibility of delays within the process. The court is empowered to extend the time limits for appeals beyond 28 days in cases where "special circumstances which make it just to do so".[264]

Scope of appeals

It is important to be clear that an appeal to the county court is a rehearing. In other words, the court is not there to review the decision of the district council but is being asked to make the decision afresh. A rehearing can allow for a range of options from a mere review of the local authority decision to a complete replacement of the decision. However,

[262] Section 68(4).

[263] Sections 68(2) & 68(3), Houses in Multiple Occupation Act (Northern Ireland) 2016.

[264] Section 67(5).

a rehearing allows the court to reconsider a decision in the fullest sense of the word, meaning "the court will hear the case again. It will if necessary hear evidence again and may well admit fresh evidence. It will reach a fresh decision unconstrained by the decision of the lower court, although it will give to the decision of the lower court the weight that it deserves."[265] This means that the original decision of the district council is largely to be cast aside and replaced by the decision of the county court. However, the county court is not an expert and, absent other expert evidence, is constrained to rely on the expertise provided to it. In England, where appeals are made to a specialist tribunal it has been held that because it contains its own specialist expertise the obligation on a court to give respect to a council decision is not binding on a specialist tribunal.[266] However, as in NI appeals are to the county court, which is not an expert Tribunal, the conclusion must be that the jurisdiction of the court is more limited than in England. As a non-expert body the Northern Ireland County Court should take into account the expertise and views of the district council unless it has good reason to depart from them.[267] Naturally, this does not mean adopting flawed reasoning but it does mean respecting the experience and expertise of a local authority and accepting, for example, that they are likely to be best placed to assess the risks inherent in specific properties based on their greater experience in the field.

---

265 *EI Du Pont De Nemours & Company v S.T. Dupont* [2003] EWCA Civ 1368 @ 96.

266 *Clark v Manchester City Council* [2015] UKUT 129 (LC).

267 *Sagnata Investments Ltd v Norwich Corporation* [1971] 2 QB 614.

CHAPTER FOURTEEN

CONCLUSIONS

Northern Ireland, as with all of the UK, is an area in which the private rented sector in particular, and the housing market in general is developing quickly. This is the case in terms of the services and accommodation styles on offer and the appetite for them.

The legislation is barely keeping pace with multiple occupancy properties, property guardians, commercial to residential conversions, build to rent serviced accommodation, online agency services, letting clubs and all the other new entrants to the market.

In some cases this is more of a nuisance in the sense of archaic legislation creating problems for modern business and preventing them achieving the efficiencies they seek. However, it has a more terrifying side as well such as where building controls fail to keep pace with new construction methods, such as cladding, leading to unanticipated fire hazards.

The devolved regions have an opportunity to apply different approaches to housing which meet their regional needs but which also allow for a range of different models to be tested. This is not to say that tenancy legislation should be a grand experiment, these are people's homes and livelihoods. However, there is scope for different legislatures to attempt to solve problems in different ways and to learn from one another. To some degree Northern Ireland has been doing just this by incorporating concepts from other parts of the UK while also developing its own ideas. Hopefully it will continue to do so.

MORE BOOKS BY LAW BRIEF PUBLISHING

'Covid-19, Homeworking and the Law – The Essential Guide to Employment and GDPR Issues' by Forbes Solicitors
'Covid-19, Force Majeure and Frustration of Contracts – The Essential Guide' by Keith Markham
'Covid-19 and Criminal Law – The Essential Guide' by Ramya Nagesh
'Covid-19 and Family Law in England and Wales – The Essential Guide' by Safda Mahmood
'A Practical Guide to the Law of Unlawful Eviction and Harassment – 2nd Edition' by Stephanie Lovegrove
'Covid-19, Residential Property, Equity Release and Enfranchisement – The Essential Guide' by Paul Sams and Louise Uphill
'Covid-19, Brexit and the Law of Commercial Leases – The Essential Guide' by Mark Shelton
'A Practical Guide to Costs in Personal Injury Claims – 2nd Edition' by Matthew Hoe
'A Practical Guide to the General Data Protection Regulation (GDPR) – 2nd Edition' by Keith Markham
'Ellis on Credit Hire – Sixth Edition' by Aidan Ellis & Tim Kevan
'A Practical Guide to Working with Litigants in Person and McKenzie Friends in Family Cases' by Stuart Barlow
'Protecting Unregistered Brands: A Practical Guide to the Law of Passing Off' by Lorna Brazell
'A Practical Guide to Secondary Liability and Joint Enterprise Post-Jogee' by Joanne Cecil & James Mehigan
'A Practical Guide to the Pre-Action RTA Claims Protocol for Personal Injury Lawyers' by Antonia Ford
'A Practical Guide to Neighbour Disputes and the Law' by Alexander Walsh
'A Practical Guide to Forfeiture of Leases' by Mark Shelton
'A Practical Guide to Coercive Control for Legal Practitioners and Victims' by Rachel Horman

'A Practical Guide to Rights Over Airspace and Subsoil' by Daniel Gatty
'Tackling Disclosure in the Criminal Courts – A Practitioner's Guide' by Narita Bahra QC & Don Ramble
'A Practical Guide to the Law of Driverless Cars – Second Edition' by Alex Glassbrook, Emma Northey & Scarlett Milligan
'A Practical Guide to TOLATA Claims' by Greg Williams
'Artificial Intelligence – The Practical Legal Issues' by John Buyers
'A Practical Guide to the Law of Prescription in Scotland' by Andrew Foyle
'A Practical Guide to the Construction and Rectification of Wills and Trust Instruments' by Edward Hewitt
'A Practical Guide to the Law of Bullying and Harassment in the Workplace' by Philip Hyland
'How to Be a Freelance Solicitor: A Practical Guide to the SRA-Regulated Freelance Solicitor Model' by Paul Bennett
'A Practical Guide to Prison Injury Claims' by Malcolm Johnson
'A Practical Guide to the Small Claims Track' by Dominic Bright
'A Practical Guide to Advising Clients at the Police Station' by Colin Stephen McKeown-Beaumont
'A Practical Guide to Antisocial Behaviour Injunctions' by Iain Wightwick
'Practical Mediation: A Guide for Mediators, Advocates, Advisers, Lawyers, and Students in Civil, Commercial, Business, Property, Workplace, and Employment Cases' by Jonathan Dingle with John Sephton
'The Mini-Pupillage Workbook' by David Boyle
'A Practical Guide to Crofting Law' by Brian Inkster
'A Practical Guide to Spousal Maintenance' by Liz Cowell
'A Practical Guide to the Law of Domain Names and Cybersquatting' by Andrew Clemson
'A Practical Guide to the Law of Gender Pay Gap Reporting' by Harini Iyengar

'A Practical Guide to the Rights of Grandparents in Children Proceedings' by Stuart Barlow
'NHS Whistleblowing and the Law' by Joseph England
'Employment Law and the Gig Economy' by Nigel Mackay & Annie Powell
'A Practical Guide to Noise Induced Hearing Loss (NIHL) Claims' by Andrew Mckie, Ian Skeate, Gareth McAloon
'An Introduction to Beauty Negligence Claims – A Practical Guide for the Personal Injury Practitioner' by Greg Almond
'Intercompany Agreements for Transfer Pricing Compliance' by Paul Sutton
'Zen and the Art of Mediation' by Martin Plowman
'A Practical Guide to the SRA Principles, Individual and Law Firm Codes of Conduct 2019 – What Every Law Firm Needs to Know' by Paul Bennett
'A Practical Guide to Adoption for Family Lawyers' by Graham Pegg
'A Practical Guide to Industrial Disease Claims' by Andrew Mckie & Ian Skeate
'A Practical Guide to Redundancy' by Philip Hyland
'A Practical Guide to Vicarious Liability' by Mariel Irvine
'A Practical Guide to Applications for Landlord's Consent and Variation of Leases' by Mark Shelton
'A Practical Guide to Relief from Sanctions Post-Mitchell and Denton' by Peter Causton
'A Practical Guide to Equity Release for Advisors' by Paul Sams
'A Practical Guide to the Law Relating to Food' by Ian Thomas
'A Practical Guide to Financial Services Claims' by Chris Hegarty
'The Law of Houses in Multiple Occupation: A Practical Guide to HMO Proceedings' by Julian Hunt
'A Practical Guide to Unlawful Eviction and Harassment' by Stephanie Lovegrove
'Occupiers, Highways and Defective Premises Claims: A Practical Guide Post-Jackson – 2nd Edition' by Andrew Mckie

'A Practical Guide to Financial Ombudsman Service Claims' by Adam Temple & Robert Scrivenor
'A Practical Guide to Advising Schools on Employment Law' by Jonathan Holden
'A Practical Guide to Running Housing Disrepair and Cavity Wall Claims: 2nd Edition' by Andrew Mckie & Ian Skeate
'A Practical Guide to Holiday Sickness Claims – 2nd Edition' by Andrew Mckie & Ian Skeate
'Arguments and Tactics for Personal Injury and Clinical Negligence Claims' by Dorian Williams
'A Practical Guide to Drone Law' by Rufus Ballaster, Andrew Firman, Eleanor Clot
'A Practical Guide to Compliance for Personal Injury Firms Working With Claims Management Companies' by Paul Bennett
'A Practical Guide to Dog Law for Owners and Others' by Andrea Pitt
'RTA Allegations of Fraud in a Post-Jackson Era: The Handbook – 2nd Edition' by Andrew Mckie
'RTA Personal Injury Claims: A Practical Guide Post-Jackson' by Andrew Mckie
'On Experts: CPR35 for Lawyers and Experts' by David Boyle
'An Introduction to Personal Injury Law' by David Boyle
'A Practical Guide to Subtle Brain Injury Claims' by Pankaj Madan

www.ingramcontent.com/pod-product-compliance
Ingram Content Group UK Ltd.
Pitfield, Milton Keynes, MK11 3LW, UK
UKHW021239300926
15471UKWH00013B/768

9 781913 715502